Cherries on a Plate

EDITED BY

MARILYN DUCKWORTH

WITH CONTRIBUTIONS FROM

ELIZABETH KNOX
FIONA FARRELL
CILLA MCQUEEN
SUE MCCAULEY
KERI HULME
MARGARET MAHY
MARILYN DUCKWORTH
FLEUR ADCOCK
RENÉE

Cherries on a Plate

New Zealand Writers Talk About Their Sisters

NEW ZEALAND LTD

Random House New Zealand Ltd
(An imprint of the Random House Group)
18 Poland Road, Glenfield
Auckland 10, NEW ZEALAND

Sydney New York Toronto
London Auckland Johannesburg
and agencies throughout the world

First published 1996
Reprinted 1996

Printed in New Zealand
ISBN 1 86941 287 7

Contents

Photographs

Acknowledgements

When I began putting this book together in 1995, I was enjoying some useful solitude in the Frank Sargeson Centre, working at the same time on a novel. My thanks are due to the Sargeson Trust for the fellowship, which made this possible.

Marilyn Duckworth

Introduction

The relationship that exists between sisters is unique, complex, sometimes problematic. The bonds can be painful. And yet when I contacted writers who might have been in this book but who had no sister, their tone was one of deepest envy and regret. A woman's longing for a child is well documented, a yearning that goes beyond the reality of broken nights and worrying responsibility. Perhaps the need for a sister is something as elemental. Certainly I feel keenly for those women who have been deprived. I am grateful that I gave birth to four daughters, who have each other. I have always had a sister. Because she is a writer like myself, she features in this book.

I have arranged these chapters more or less chronologically, approximately according to age. Thus Elizabeth Knox, at thirty-seven, opens the book. She is the only middle sister contributing and chooses to write not from childhood forward but about a time when, newly adult, she and her sisters shared a flat in the Wellington suburb of Brooklyn. At 'home' she had seen herself and her younger sister Sara as 'contents under pressure' — in the Reuben Avenue flat that pressure escapes.

Six of the women writing here are first-born, which gives rise to some poignant observations on how it feels to be 'replaced'. 'Obviously I had not come up to their expectations,' mourns Fleur Adcock. She goes on, 'The world is full of first-born children behaving badly to their younger rivals.' One thinks of Keri Hulme blandly encouraging her sister to walk on hot ashes. Margaret Mahy, the eldest of four, was overjoyed at the births of her sisters but confesses to a later urge 'to dominate Helen, but she refused to be dominated'. She notes worriedly that the eldest is 'doomed by the determinism of fairy tales to make wrong choices'. Cilla McQueen says simply of Ali, four years her junior, 'I was mean to her sometimes'. Renée — 'I am the eldest, therefore I am the boss' — loves and envies her little sister, goes so far as throttling Val's teddy bear, Edward.

Sue McCauley and myself are younger sisters, so a different dynamic prevails. Perhaps because, like her and Fiona Farrell, I am an only sister, I can't help believing that this is the more intense experience. My own sister Fleur writes: 'to be one of two sisters accounts for some of the most violent, passionate and savage emotions a young human being is capable of'. But the difference between being an older or a younger sister is something I can only dimly apprehend. Sue McCauley feels admiration and pride for the sister who went ahead of her, which I understand. When they were growing up, she criticised her sister for being 'intrinsically nice' and spent her childhood aiming to be different; in middle age she wants 'to have been like her'. This pull and tug between the need for difference is interesting. Sisters share their sex, their parents and usually their childhood environment. Differences that grow out of this sameness can loom large and surprising. But similarities can be surprising, too, by turns irritating and reassuring, to be denied one day and reclaimed the next. Sisterly resemblances and affinities are both constricting and comforting, like love itself.

Fiona Farrell, aware of this from an early age, writes: 'We maintained careful differences: she liked sago and hated roly-poly. I hated sago and loved roly-poly.' As students at university, Fiona confesses that she and her sister quarrelled bitterly, wanted 'to stop being sisters, wanting to be our single, mysterious selves'. Exactly. Every sister knows what she means. Keri Hulme (indubitably a single, mysterious self) lists characteristics she shares with her sisters — 'short-sightedness; a deep sense of justice (what is right, tika, fair play)' — but comfortably owns up to huge differences. 'I am extraordinarily self-sufficient, and my sisters . . . need other people for happiness.'

It becomes clear that the sister bond persists across oceans and indeed beyond the grave. Only Cook Strait separates Sue McCauley from her sister, while Cilla McQueen's sisters are separated from her by the Pacific or by the length of Aotearoa. Elizabeth Knox and Fiona Farrell's sisterly telephone calls must cross the Tasman, while Fleur and I occupy different hemispheres most of the time. Only Keri Hulme and Margaret Mahy breathe the same air as their sisters, that of South Island New Zealand. Keri talks to her sisters every week and claims family as the most important factor in her life. 'Take away my family . . . take away my sisters, and there is very little *me* left . . .'

The nine contributors to this collection have chosen different approaches. These have little to do with their position in the family, more, perhaps, to do with their particular skills as writers. Cilla McQueen, poet, writes hers in conjunction with her sisters, as a play for three voices, backgrounded by her own poet's sensibility. Keri Hulme's distinctive rhythms of speech sing powerfully, sometimes in te reo Māori. Renée, playwright and novelist, presents her sister and herself with a dramatist's flair and use of dialogue, at times extending her cast to the whole family. Margaret Mahy, irrepressible entertainer of young people, offers a fantasy opening in which her sisters introduce themselves but in the eldest sister's chosen words. Margaret 'tried to organise the family imagination' from early in her life and continues to do so here, sensitively and wittily. Fiona Farrell shares her piece more literally with her sister Moira, giving due acknowledgement to the role now played by the telephone, linking them across the Tasman.

My sister Fleur and I are the only two writers here who have to bear witness against, or for, each other. I insisted that we write our contributions without collusion and we later read the other's with nervous curiosity. It was a relief to find that we didn't make liars of each other and yet, aside from some interesting overlapping, they are very different accounts.

Dreams, or more accurately, nightmares, live and become legendary in the minds of children. Fleur and I remember each other's sympathetically. Cilla McQueen and her sisters recall her 'Lucky Hag' dream, when a witch came out of the linen cupboard. Games and songs and rituals recur like a motif in most of these accounts. The most complex and interesting of these, taped and transcribed, is Elizabeth Knox's 'the game', which she sees as 'pretty dodgy therapy' for one sister; for herself it 'had to be art, to be my workshop'. It's

tempting to see these recurring inventive games as part of the training ground for being a writer, but this would be a simplification. It was Sue McCauley's sister who invented their game, 'Native People' — 'a semi-stone age soap opera'. As children, Fiona and Moira Farrell celebrated 'Giggle Nights' and 'There is still something of the Giggle Night when we talk on the phone.' Margaret Mahy and her sisters happily remember how to 'sing the old songs, repeat the words of old nonsense games'. Keri Hulme and her sisters go fishing with Tinkerbell in Never-never Land. Fleur and I retain hand-written stories of Dreamland and our own ritual nonsense. Renée is reminded of how she directed her sister in a toetoe dance which, if it wasn't done correctly, resulted in a belting with the toetoe. Renée's sister died in 1992 and her contribution is affectionate, moving, but pulls no punches.

These are real stories about real people, vivid characters, sometimes sharper than fiction. Brothers, mothers and even fathers are allowed their bit parts in the text. As well as pleasure, there is usually something raw and uncomfortable about remembering honestly, but this is what the women in this book have done. Stories, games, rituals and nightmares weave in and out of the reminiscences, sewing sisters together into a tight, rich cloth that no outsider would dare to unstitch.

Marilyn Duckworth,
Wellington 1996

ELIZABETH KNOX

Reuben Avenue

Elizabeth Knox, novelist and essayist, was born in Wellington, New Zealand, in 1959. Her novel *After Z-Hour* won the PEN Best First Book of Prose Award in 1988 and her second novel *Treasure* was shortlisted for the New Zealand Book Award for fiction in 1993. Her latest novel, *The Glamour and the Sea,* has just been published by Victoria University Press. In addition, she has published two novellas, *Paremata* and *Pomare.* She lives in Wellington with her husband and son.

Sara and I left home in May 1980. We got off a train at Wellington railway station and trekked to the ANZ on Lambton Quay, put down our packs and waited for ten, the bank opening hour. There was no mistaking us for backpackers. The packs were Dad's, and old, one an A-frame climbing pack with his address on its top flap: 'R. A. Knox, Guides' Quarters, The Hermitage, Mount Cook.' The other was a tramping pack, a stiff box of mummified canvas, gritty, and the colour of the dry earth under the house where it had been stored. Sara and I sat on the pavement against a plate-glass window and sang, 'You don't — have — to live like a refugee.'

The day before, Sunday, a friend had loaded the tray of a borrowed truck with Mum's two ex-government chairs (serial numbers branded on their arms), bookshelves, coffee table, boxed books, bedding in plastic sacks. I rode with the friend from Paremata to Brooklyn and the top of Reuben Avenue. Sara arrived with Dad, our hundred-and-forty-dollar stereo and the record collection. I remember that Dad was quiet and sour. It must have looked like troop movements. All his daughters were off at once, Sara and I for the first time and Mary for her third stab at flatting. Mary's comings and goings from her several unsuccessful flats only disguised all of us making a break for it. Did Dad realise that I had waited with Sara till she finished her sixth form and got her first job? That she'd asked me to stay to help her live with his drinking? Did he understand that our leaving left Mum at home without her mistaken obligation to 'keep home together for the kids'?

Dad was silent, possibly hung over; it's hard to determine from memory, because around that time I'd given up looking at his face.

On Monday Sara and I reached the top of Reuben Avenue by eleven. Our beds arrived in a furniture store delivery truck. Two new single beds — Mum had bought them as a house-warming gift. We had thought we could take our own, which was like a declaration, that we'd never spend another night at Paremata. A week before we left Mum informed us: 'You can't take those beds, because they don't belong to you.' I offered to buy them. One of our clashes.

Mum's stands were usually more constructive than mine — and showed a greater appreciation of the vicissitudes of life. It wasn't that she was hanging onto the chattels because her home had bust up, she was just hiding the matches from her bridge-burning daughters, showing the same clever husbandry that had made her hide certain books from us girls when we were younger — Havelock Ellis's *Studies in the Psychology of Sex* from Mary, Poe's *Tales of Mystery and Imagination* from me. Mum showed no strong feelings about our tendencies, only seemed to do what anyone attentive remembers to do with heliotropic houseplants: turn them occasionally to keep them growing straight.

When the beds arrived Sara and I set up house. The flat — number 61 — was shaped like an L with a stubby foot. It was one of several free-standing units that stepped up the slope between the street's last old cottage and a Brooklyn Hill colonial farmhouse, high above the street and concealed by an honour guard of macrocarpas. We were thirty steps up the flight that led on from the top of a street so steep that I had to stop wearing the high heels I'd bought when I'd got my second full-time job. Even in three-inch heels I had to tackle the slope backwards.

For the first few weeks our flat felt like another country. Brooklyn had variations on weather I never knew elsewhere in Wellington. For instance — fog. There were days when we could stand on the wet lap of lawn behind our flat and listen to people talking some distance off — voices carried, tone and pitch perfectly preserved, through the particles of water vapour, as if by some kind of osmotic pressure. Sometimes I came home out of fog so thick that the flat felt like a sealed capsule of clear air, and *submerged* — not the eyrie it was.

There were three bedrooms, two of a good size, and one small bedroom that we not only never used, but that later somehow seemed to become *outside*, and was occupied by outsiders. A month after we had moved in, one female possum and her two suitors found their way into our ceiling through a gap under the header tank. From their point of entry they could proceed in two directions — into the warm gallery between the ceiling and roof, or through a gap between the studs and out the unclad walls of the toilet. First Sara and I were kept up all night by a bowling alley racket of frisky possums, then Sara opened the toilet door one morning to confront a possum perched on the cistern, staring pop-eyed and witless. The landlord's agent came, unbuckled her bike jacket, put her hands on her hips and organised us 'girls'. If we could vacate the premises for a few hours she'd put a borer bomb in the ceiling — that should sort them out.

They were back the following night. The agent hadn't properly replaced the hatch to the roof. In the middle of their romping some possum made a mis-step, and discovered a new world. There was a downpour that day, just as I got off the bus by the Brooklyn shops. By the time I reached our back door the water was through the shoulder seams of my coat, and my hair was wet to the scalp. My fingers were white and stiff, and as I struggled to fit the key into the lock I happened to glance sideways at the window of the small bedroom and saw a possum sitting on the windowsill — a warm, dry possum. Sara heard my key and when the door didn't open she opened it herself to find me standing, laughing. When we investigated the bedroom we found two possums, and the ceiling hatch smashed on the floor of the wardrobe. The animals didn't even have the decency to bolt. They just hopped back into the wardrobe and stood like they were waiting for a bus.

I reclaimed the toilet by stuffing an old sheet in between the studs and gib-board. But for several days, whenever I sat on the toilet I heard them digging at the blockage. I'd bang on the walls and listen to the scrubbing brush sound of a hairy animal turning in a small space.

This invasion was just the sort of situation our father would normally sort out, but when we rang him he didn't show any interest in our problem, or concern. And when we asked to speak to Mum, she was out. For two days she was out. Then she rang me from the Forest Service, where she worked. I was tending the Gestetner in the printing department at Butterworths. Past my protective earphones I felt the telephone's bell as a vibration that plumped out the loud rhythms of the printing machine. I disengaged various rollers and switched off the air-pump. The machine marked time while I took the receiver around the doorframe to talk. Mum wondered whether I'd like to go to *La Bohème* with her that evening. She didn't think it was Sara's cup of tea.

'Aren't you going with Dad?'

'It's his ticket I'm offering you. There's no sense in wasting it. I've left him.'

She was staying with our youngest aunt. Perhaps Sara and I would like to come up for dinner, then she and I could go to the opera.

Mum was sleeping in the sunporch of Shona's flat. Sara noticed that she'd bought herself an alarm clock. We had to take *that* seriously. It appeared that Mum had waited for us to leave home and, at last entitled to bargain only for herself, had issued her ultimatum: Stop drinking or I'll leave. He didn't, and she did. When she went to fetch her coat and put on lipstick, Sara and I had a quick consultation. We must rescue the cats; Dad couldn't be trusted to take care of the cats. But how was it possible to relocate the seventeen-year-old? Mum came back and we headed down town. Mum put Sara in a taxi at Courtenay Place and then we walked on to the Opera House.

Tissue-paper snow. Mimi's pathetic self-assertion.

Sara and I took a break from the Gordons, had our hands stamped and walked out of the Thistle Hall. The music went on, hummed through our heads, from ear to ear, like an arterial road in rush hour.

We went to the Taj for coffee and cake. Sara got out some scrap paper to write notes for her *Rip-it-Up* review. What did I think?

A woman in a hand-painted silk scarf leaned across the table and said to her date, 'Haven't those girls got lower-class Kiwi accents?'

Sara started doing her London punks, Johnny Rotten on whatever record company: '*Sometimes* they give us *problems*.' We had a quick look at the paintings, and Sara said, with haughty authority, 'Not much worth looking at in here.'

Sara was a connoisseur of beauty — of boyish girls and pretty boys. When she and her friend Neil came back from a Gary Numan concert she was pale and prim of lip, like she got with menstrual cramps. Neil sat down beside me and said, 'I could die of embarrassment.' Sara went into the bedroom; then there was a crash. We ran in to find her lying on the floor between the beds, howling.

'What happened?' I asked.

'Oh for God's sake!' Neil was disgusted.

The duvet had pulled, obliquely, off the bed. Its corner lay under her. I replayed the crash and realised she'd cast herself onto her bed in tears — and missed.

'He was so beautiful,' she mourned. 'I'll never see him again.'

'She can't mean Gary Numan,' I said to Neil.

'No. There was a cute boy at the concert. And she had to tell him he was beautiful.'

I watched the little muscles work around Neil's eyes. We started to laugh.

'But Sara,' I said, 'you don't even go for boys.'

'He was wearing a soft red shirt and white jeans with a thin black belt. His eyebrows were fine and expressive. His profile — narrow high cheekbones, smooth skin, slightly jutting lips . . .' Her inventory of desirables.

Sara did this, got crushes and wrote poetry about beautiful young people, or glimpsed bodies. In her ruled school exercise books were pages with round raised patches where tears had fallen and the blue lines blurred. It made me furious; it was silly and, I'd tell her, couldn't she see she was getting hung up on inessentials? But beauty was an essential to Sara (and later, when her tastes became more sophisticated, that ineffable, *style*). She used to say she'd have given anything to be beautiful.

Three days after the concert and six after the opera, Mum and Dad turned up at our flat. Mary was there too. When Sara and I inspected 61 Reuben Avenue before signing the lease, we learned that 63 would soon be empty. Mary wasn't about to be left behind at Paremata, and was now our neighbour. She had brought over a tin of the jaw-breaking kibbled wheat cookies which she baked although only I liked them. Sara was limping about with the head of the broom tucked into her armpit. She'd twisted something exercising, and had just abandoned her initial pretence of sweeping the floor. She sat at the knock on the door, and put the broom down — but its handle had already made a shotgun scattering of little pits in our brittle lino.

Dad's face was in the process of being remodelled by contrition. He looked like someone relaxing out of a

prolonged headache. He said he was stopping drinking. I said, oh yeah, I liked that, 'stopping', not 'stopped'. He'd been a fool, he said, had never really grown up. Sara patted him on the arm. Mary, wary, said, 'Well, that's good' — she said it a couple of times. I stood with the table between me and my parents and sobbed with rage — if that was all it took, why didn't she leave him earlier, instead of obliging us to live besieged, ashamed, with poison pouring in our ears day and night for years? How many times had I begged him to stop drinking — when all the time it was in her power, and she didn't use her power.

Sara was angry with me. She said I should just be grateful and gracious. But Mary, who scarcely ever did those things, came and put her arms around me.

Sara limped into the kitchen to make Dad a cup of tea — talked through the hatch to him about our four-recipe flat menu: spaghetti, new goob soup, old goob soup, and aeroplane glue rice. Mum began to prowl, opened the door of the possum room. Hadn't we had them trapped and removed? The man two flats down had friends at Dalgety's. He'd caught the culprits over three nights — first he'd set the trap in the ceiling and we had to listen to its magnified steely rattle all night.

'Poor things,' said Dad. I told him that possums were too stupid to despair.

Mum wanted to know why we hadn't cleaned up the possum poo.

It was too soft to vacuum and there was no way we were going to pick up the whole lot by hand, Sara said. 'We'll let it dry for a while before vacuuming.' Sara could make anything sound like good sense. When she was a child everyone agreed she was practical — because she ate while the rest of us argued, and because she made machines that worked with her Meccano. Kids like to be characterised by praise — so Sara was practical, Mary imaginative, and I was good.

As I said, there were three bedrooms in our flat. Yet when we moved in Sara and I put Mum's house-warming beds in one room, the only way they'd fit, parallel, with their heads against the curtained window. We carried on as we had for the last ten years, playing our imaginary game.

If you put your ear to the bedroom door, as Mary sometimes did the following year when she came to live with us (and we would know she was listening only when she laughed at our jokes), you would perhaps hear something like this:

Me (childish, disaffected): 'I want a friend,' Creare says. 'Supply me with one. Why don't we get a town house? Why do we have to build this stupid house in the middle of nowhere?'

Sara: 'Who are you talking to?' Vlad asks, and puts a hand on her head.

Me: 'All of you. I'd like a whole list of friends I could invite. Kids my age. I could ask Jasmine, but it's a long way for her to come without her mother. And I don't know anybody in Garaven. Why does my father have to only ever know reprobates, criminals and renegades — and nobody respectable with a family?'

I've transcribed from one of the few tapes we made. There's a cicada sawing away in the background, so it's late summer. The tape is captioned 251/2L/73 — the two-hundred-and-fifty-first day of the second year in the reign of the seventy-third queen of Avernum. (To study Avernumite history every Acturan has first to know how long each queen lived, and that a total of seven years of rule by two usurpers are not to be counted.) Listening to the tape, I know that, if a cicada was singing, and it was the second year of Minx's reign and the brethren had just built Cryheron, then Sara and I were still at Paremata.

You get the picture. I shared a room with my younger sister to play an imaginary game, to advance a plot — not so that we could *be ourselves*, but so that we could be *them*.

We worked hard at the game in 1979 and 1980. Our friend Carol had left the game in a state of hypovolemic shock. Mary felt discouraged and all but gave it up. Between us, Sara and I nursed the story back to life. Various people emigrated, closed bank accounts, bought real estate, married, learned new trades. There was no flight, exile, amnesia — all that came later, when things got tougher and more estranged.

Now, whenever we — Sara and I — write about the game, to move forward at all we have to make a great effort against the inertia of its oddness, which is the oddness of a thing that both happens, like life, so has contingencies; and is shaped, like art, so has order. To talk about the game we must first say what it was, then represent, in a short form, how it worked. It is possible to give a sense of scale even without facts and figures. (Faked imaginary worlds in books are transparent, as public and penetrable as fiction.) If, without any attempt to elucidate, I remark on the difficulty with dates and the discipline of history in Acturus, I offer some sense of scale. For the story wasn't about historians or bankers or dressmakers — but I can give you names; or about soldiers, sea captains, poets, priestesses, experts in etiquette, cooks or explorers — but I can give you names. And with every name I can offer all or some of a biography, from whole life histories to single encounters.

Once what-it-was and how-it-worked are established (you don't have to understand, just extrapolate a great real thing, as scientists do giant squid from the dinner plate-sized sucker marks on the heads of Cook Strait sperm whales), then I can try to say how we *felt* about the game.

In 1980, when we — Mary, Sara, and I — thought about the game we were all in error. We loved, were entertained and sustained by our imaginary game, but had the wrong ideas about it.

Sara knew it had preserved her self-respect, given her a chance to explore thoughts and feelings about the world, and about sexuality, that would have been painful and difficult if it was herself, her history and identity, doing the exploring. At ten Sara had been sexually abused by an old man who lived up the road from us. Her absorption in the game was, in part, a retreat from that — and deferred various troubles till she was older and better equipped to deal with them. The game was pretty dodgy therapy, but it did make a difference, and it was — to use the right language — self-directed.

The game was my hermitage. I was thirteen when Sara came to me for help — I won't write about that here, but to say that the adult world which rolled out before me then, like a carpet made of blood and bruises, was clearly not a safe place for a soul to be. Still, I did want the world. I had to take the good things I'd learned, and made, into the bad place I saw and — you know — *redeem* it. At sixteen I worked out that I should be some kind of artist. A *real* writer, I decided. My imaginary game must be art too, to be my workshop. And I wasn't prepared to be extraordinary on my own — my sisters had to be pilgrims as well, come with me to carry the baggage. They had to have the right mental attitudes and read the right books . . . By twenty-one — even with the possums, old goob soup, the dark nail polish hiding the printer's ink under my nails — I was a hero. A hero and a bully.

I'm not sure how Mary thought about the game. I'll make a guess. Mary got ideas into her head that evidence and circumstances, even her own feelings, moved only with great difficulty. She seemed to think that it was proper for her to stop playing because Carol had. She said it was all too sad and she couldn't imagine a future for them — or not a cheerful future. She was the oldest and maybe thought it was time to get on with the business of life. No provisions were made for her. When that crew who later came to be known as the Cryheron Brethren packed their bags, picked up their kids and rode out of Avergild, all they said to Mary's main character Thomasina was goodbye, maybe they'd write.

Sara and I, wrapped up in ourselves, were always careless of Mary. But it was hard to know what she felt. Her feelings seemed blockaded behind various ideas (never dogma, she wouldn't take the usual line on anything). How to explain this. The Knox girls were all blockheads, but Mary had *enthusiasms* — Greece, Islam, natural childbirth. They were all reasonable and authentic, but she bombarded her intimates with them. She never seemed to notice that you weren't returning her serves, that she wasn't having a conversation. A whiteout of tennis balls, that's what it was like — you would end up bruised, buried and obscured from her view. But she was *good* at the conversations she had, she would listen then come up, surprisingly, from under the surface of a discussion. (The only sports prizes she won at school were for swimming underwater — she had lung capacity, and no apparent need of audible applause.)

People in their early twenties usually feel a need to decide how to be. My sisters made their moves at Reuben Avenue. I had already made mine.

In 1979, when I was twenty, I'd spent ten months living on money saved from two years as a basic grade clerk in the IRD at Porirua. I wrote a novel, *One Too Many Lives*, about four girls with an imaginary game. David Elworthy, the publisher at Collins, thought hard about publishing it — but they could afford only one novel that year and they took (wisely) Philip Temple's *Beak of the Moon*. Sorry to disappoint me, Elworthy then acted as an agent, and sent the book, with a recommendation, to several publishers in England. They were all either gentle, or encouraging, but none took it. This was just as well, as it was an 'apprentice piece', and very

young. An editor at Gollancz who liked it a lot couldn't decide whether it was adults' or young adults' fiction, which seemed at the time a slight to the novel. There were conflicting opinions as to why the book didn't 'work', explained with varying degrees of wit and learning. The consensus was that it was odd — oddly odd — and a freak at first sight is always a cripple, never a prodigy.

I was hurt, and determined to try again. 'Next time,' I thought, as I banked my redundancy cheque from Butterworths, a cheque that took my account to $3,500, when this time my budget target of savings-on-which-to-write-a-novel was $5,000, 'Next time I'll write a novel with no weird stuff, a novel about society, with politics and love troubles . . .'

There was a problem with my plan. When I had my $5,000 I might not have the house all to myself during the day. Mary had suffered a succession of flatmate troubles, and she'd had to resign from another job (she had quit or been fired from a total of eight, by then). She made noises about moving in with me and Sara. We didn't want her. It was nice having her handy, next door, and the cats we'd acquired, Mary's white Luke and our black Taan, roosting together in the rain in the disused chicken coop behind the flat. We would come home together, call them and see them separate like a bright body and its shadow, Luke trotting after Mary and Taan looping through the long grass, chirping on each downbeat, to our door.

Sara and I had our cool pursuits, the concerts, and writing for the rock magazine. We were crazy, had been 'contents under pressure' in the family home with our father, under curfew after the sixth drink, silent in the family room, or shut in our bedroom. At Reuben Avenue we read each other poetry — Yeats, Keats and Tennyson. 'Beneath all fancied hopes and fears / Ay me, the sorrow deepens down, / Whose muffled motions blindly drown / The bases of my life in tears.'

Or we made jokes till we had indigestion. We'd stay up to twelve playing our imaginary game then get into duels of limericks late, very late, and Sara would always win:

There once was a fellow from Kent
Whose prick was terrifically bent
He'd stick it round corners
At grief-stricken mourners
Who couldn't quite see what he meant.

On walks or while I was cooking, Sara would start being these 'fun' characters she had: the punks, manic Terry and morose Jerry; the SS man Heinz Von Tockentau trying to question an obtuse Dutch resistance fighter who would keep going on about his 'vife Fru', in 'de vindmill'; or she'd be Chauncy Beauregarde of Seven Oaks (or six-and-a-half since his grandpappy chopped one down); or the hick from Arkansas who saw Abraham Lincoln shot in the 'thee-ay-ay-ta'. I'd laugh till my stomach ached. I can remember one night standing outside in the cold watching a lunar eclipse (the moon went a dull, sullen red), laughing so much at Sara's antics that slobber was running out of my mouth.

And we were squalid. For three months in winter the drying weather was so bad that Sara didn't bother to wash her

sheets and pyjamas. Her night attire rotted, and her sheet was ripped by her long toenails. Washing soured in the machine; mildew crept down the bathroom walls like nightfall. We talked and talked — we'd let ourselves go.

What Sara and I did, to dodge Mary's occupancy, was to advertise a room. Sara put up a notice at polytech. After one interview we came to — who in their right mind would want to live with us?

The young woman who turned up to look the flat over arrived with her mother, who I remember standing at the door to 'the possum room' looking at the oily blotches the drying droppings had left on the carpet. We explained, and she seemed bemused and dubious. If she had exhibited shock it would have been harder to see ourselves from her point of view, as it was I think we felt we should explain rather than apologise. (The mother — who stepped back as I shut the door to the possum room, and listened attentively to my story about how our inside had become an outside and unmanageable — was Marilyn Duckworth.)

Mary moved in. The third bedroom quickly became a mess, then a midden. She and Sara squabbled about each other's domestic methods — how to cook black pudding, how much water to use washing the kitchen floor. Mary was there to mind the flat, and feed our cat when we wanted to spend the weekend at Paremata. We shook our heads together when she went out in one of her ensembles — say — Charlie Blacks, white socks, grey sweat pants, grey polo neck with red stripes, and *over this* a brown pinafore dress and a green coat.

To Sara it was all evidence for an argument. 'No wonder we don't know anyone,' she'd say. 'Everyone thinks there's something *wrong* with us.'

'How does it follow,' I'd say, 'that we don't know anyone, but do know what everyone thinks?'

'You know what I mean.'

I didn't really. I'd postponed the worry, the world. *One Too Many Lives* came back from publishers and I wrote my plausible book, *Salamander*. I wrote without enjoyment, exacting evocations of the limited possibilities of life in an office backroom; speculations about family history, drinking and fate; a story of unrequited love; the Springbok Tour, and a government playing with rugby matches near combustible public opinion. And, while I wrote, I watched the very fair, arteriosclerotic old man across the way creep about his wet garden; and his wife, who was too ill to go out, appear sometimes as a gauzy pinkness behind the bathroom window. I listened to the German shepherd down the road whine in lonely anxiety, and to the kids in the grounds of the school across the valley making their periodic din, day after day. I ignored my fight or flight impulse, persisted in a doomed enterprise, never in danger of my life — but still, I couldn't ride for more than thirty minutes on a train or bus without feeling sweaty, faint and sick; and when my doctor made me stand on his scales he told me off.

Once, when our gloomy older cousin was over for dinner he talked about the problem of *living* life and *being* someone. How he put it was that doing any particular thing seemed a sellout of the possibility of making ultimate statements.

There were only particular things, I argued (and held my stomach). 'There's only the task in front of you. Whether you're thinking about destiny or just a future there's only ever this thing, and the next and the next.'

'And the next and the next — then finally the exit,' said Mary. 'Note that she thinks it's all in sequence.'

'If you're thinking of doing anything you have to think in sequence.'

'You say that because you write novels,' said Sara.

Our cousin asked, 'What good does it do? Completing tasks. It's like shouting into a grave.'

I told him I'd let him know what good it did in ten or twenty years.

If there were times when Sara and I worried about what we saw as Mary's incompetence, or I worried about what I saw as Sara's self-destructiveness, there were things *I* did that must have given my sisters cause to worry.

One night Sara and I set off down Reuben Avenue to watch *Apocalypse Now* at the Penthouse. I'd been in all week, apart from shopping expeditions, and the writing had been going badly. There was a sudden cloudburst, and I stopped, told Sara I couldn't breathe. It was like being underwater. I wanted to go back home. Sara stood staring at me with her jacket held up over her head — a baleful hunchback. Then she said, 'Oh for God's sake!' And walked away from me.

I climbed back up the hill through rain like (it seemed to me) a force field, or glass prison bars.

Mary wrapped a blanket around me, sat me in the bean

bag, made me sweet tea and listened as I found my way out of the sound loop I'd been caught in since she opened the door. 'I couldn't tell which way was up and which was down.' My teeth chattered. I stopped repeating myself. 'Nothing was familiar. I didn't know whether I'd end up here or somewhere else. If I didn't go where I'd been most recently I wouldn't get there, or anywhere.'

I remember looking into Mary's eyes (she was helping me hold the mug) and asking, peevish, 'When will these things stop happening to me?'

In autumn of 1982 Mary placed an ad in the paper, advertised herself as a 'small, talkative blonde'. She collected seventy replies and we, Mary and I, sat on the living room floor, read the letters and sorted them into piles — yes, no, and maybe. There were eleven in the 'yes' pile. She made phone calls and dates with eight or so, was out every night of the week and full of stories about the awkward moment of decision on a second cup of coffee, the keen one who walked her to the bus, this one pleasant and insufficient, this other weirdo who went on about some blood-drinking murderer from Dusseldorf.

Sara's face appeared in the kitchen hatchway. Till now Mary's seventy suitors had been an embarrassment about which Sara said no one must know. But she wanted a full description of this guy, who must have been talking about Peter Kurten.

There was one short letter in green ballpoint that Mary kept fishing out of the 'maybe' pile. Perhaps she liked its self-

respecting diffidence — that's what I recall I noticed. Anyway, she rang the maybe man and came back from their meeting enlivened. He was bossy, she said, and some of his opinions were a bit cobwebbed, but he was interesting and she hadn't had to make an effort to listen to him. 'My eyes didn't water — you know what I mean?'

Three weeks later they were engaged. I was surprised, because it was sudden and Mary had reported him as saying he wasn't the marrying kind (a remark which, if made in the first months of any relationship, I now know means someone is thinking of making, or dreaming of accepting . . .).

Sara regarded the proposal as vindication of all the Knox sisters — why, if it was possible for *unstylish* Mary, then things could happen for us too. How long after this it was that Sara stood in a newsagent's copying down the address of a singles contact magazine, I don't know. Those months were as rushed as a mailout. But Sara did write away, browsed the lists of couples wanting a third and picked out a 'bi-girl seeking another for fun times'.

Mary moved in with her fiancé. Sara went to training college for the second module of her New Zealand Library Certificate. She got bronchitis, but didn't find time out from study to visit the doctor, until, after a night awake listening to the fluid growl in her chest, I hid all her shoes and forced her to make and keep an appointment.

I finished the novel on a day so cold I could see my breath indoors — a sunny day, but at eleven the dew still wasn't dry. At noon the sun went from the room I wrote in. I disliked my novel, had no pleasure writing it, and the moment I pulled the last page from my portable, split the original and carbon and laid them on the top of the two face-down piles of pages, I knew my 'task' was a casket.

It was spring when Sara arrived home one evening in the bi-girl's shiny deodorised car, came in looking bleak and said, 'So much hair — must have huge tap-roots in her head.' Then she asked me to give this woman the brush-off when she called. 'Just tell her I don't want to see her.'

I was relieved it was over. We could put it behind us. Novels, and the dishonour lists of photocopied singles mags. We could get on with our game. It had paused for Mary's wedding plans, my final chapters, Sara's last stint of study. We hadn't planned our next moves (their next moves). Paused, my ideas about the characters' futures seemed to turn into a real future and the whole thing into a history, so that Starfire, standing at the window of Cryheron watching his daughter on the beach in the evening, burying her legs in the sand to keep the sandflies from biting, was thinking how he must make her an orphan and, before that, dispossess her completely by sending her away to Caer Vayporo, where she wouldn't be a target for his enemies. While, on the beach, little Creare tried to live with her vision of, in twenty years' time, stopping in the marketplace of Garaven to watch a puppeteer play out, in a marionette theatre, the lives and deaths of all the people she loves.

It was from a sense of these sad contingencies, and a fear of my own ability to go on ticking off the boxes of my own tasks *ad infinitum*, and out of the ordinary obligations of an older sister who was *listening* (Sara said, about the singles

magazine, 'What else could I do? I can't help being bad'), that I gave up my reprieve. I agreed to fob off the bi-girl. But Sara must see that she shouldn't put herself in the position of hating or distrusting someone she meant to sleep with. 'You have to be honest, and get out of the closet.'

There was a Women's Resource Centre in town. I bowled in several days later and sought advice. I was given the number of a woman from the last 'coming-out group' who was about to initiate another.

'You'll go to the group a bit, meet other lesbians, then graduate, I guess,' I said to Sara after filling her in. 'And apparently I'm not supposed to push you.'

Sara had recently completed her homework for library school, a bibliographic project, its subject 'Homosexuality'. She had read a lot of books, and the best ones recommended that *she pick up that phone*. So she picked up the phone.

On the Monday of Labour Weekend, 1982, Sara and I were at Paremata. The TV was on and Dad was in and out from the kitchen tending his artichoke soup and scoffing at a local arts programme. Over breakfast he'd persuaded me not to try to rewrite the novel; to just put it away. I had sat with my head in my hands, crying and asking, 'What am I going to do?' Mum said, 'We think you should go to university.'

We were due back at the flat that night — for work on Tuesday. On the way in we would stop in to borrow a Victoria University Calendar from some friends. On the phone they told us about a flat they had found, five minutes from the campus — perhaps we would like to discuss sharing?

Sara was reading *The Circle*, a lesbian magazine with cathartic short stories about hets with handbags rescued from rapists by axe-swinging amazons. Dad sailed back into the room waving a knife flecked with parsley and, after watching the TV for another minute, announced that the most effective form of anti-intellectualism was to let idiots run a programme in celebration of the arts. Outside it began to hail, hard. Dad said he hoped Mum was in the garage. A moment later she came up the path, with hail bouncing off the yellow bucket she held over her head.

I vacuumed away the last of the dried foam of carpet shampoo. The marks of the possum droppings were as faint now as leaf shadows the moment before a cloud covers the sun and all shadows vanish.

'Do you think we've ever spent, in total, more than a couple for hours in this room?' I asked Sara. 'And we paid rent for it.'

'I never liked this room. It was unhealthy. The whole flat was,' Sara said. Then, 'I'm not going to lead an unhealthy life any more. You know, I have real difficulty explaining my life to Jenny and Caren and Snoop and Jude. No assumed common ground.'

'You should be proud of your weird life, even if it's hard to transmit.'

'Well, Elizabeth, it's easy for you. You don't mind being seen as weird and serious. But I want to have a turn at being *young*.'

In a family, to be 'serious' is to be the one who is made responsible for others' well-being. I intercepted Sara when — after I *knew* — I caught her on her way up the road to visit the old man. 'What are you doing?' I'd say, and order her back indoors. (And was never afterwards blind to the deep-sea monster shape beneath 'I can't help being bad'.) When she drained the brake fluid from Dad's car I jogged to the local garage, bought some and replaced it with the little funnel the mechanic sold me.

Once Dad drove off the road because he had cramp in his leg and, as the car ticked and others blew past, he explained to me ('You must understand . . .') why he had resumed drinking this time, to tide him over a bad patch. My only options were to ask him not to, or say I understood. Dad could report, when Mum went back to him, that perhaps he'd never really grown up — after years of teasing her about how 'grown up' she was, timidly wedded to order, about her bourgeois love of fine things, her niceties, her prejudices against plain speaking or eating offal. Of course this is a version of an available national myth. The refined woman wants her man to give up his wrecker's yard, but it's his roots, his independence, his true self.

(The fact is that only those of us who are careful are open to charges of acting against nature. Because, regardless of our efforts, the universe is cooling, and dust collects even in closed rooms.)

Sara still rings me for advice, in order to orient herself with my thoughts on what she should or shouldn't do. But periodically she tells me that her friends say that she places far too much weight on my opinions. What Elizabeth thinks about what Sara does is a quality in Sara's life like the still water behind a dam — it sits in reserve, heavy but *back there*. As to particulars — good angels make white noise, who ever hears what they have to say? And my ardour is like a harelip, a deformity that mars my diction.

Mum and Dad left Paremata for a smaller house, though not a 'retirement community' with cycle paths for motorised trikes. They have youth at hand — teenagers on one side of them, a baby on the other. Dad resettled his belongings, reroofed the garage, made repairs. Mum started another garden.

My older sister Mary has been married thirteen years to the man from the maybe pile. They have two daughters. Reuben Avenue was the last place we lived together.

Sara is home from Melbourne for Christmas. She has just finished her PhD, *Doing Violence: The Meaning of Murder in Post-War American Culture*. We are at our parents' place in Raumati. She comes into the living room, where her nephew has lined up all his Kirk's plastic wildlife for a formal introduction to the new one, a Nile crocodile. Sara asks Dad if she can borrow his vice. And his hole-punch, and the basement workshop for a while. She has a bag of rivets, and black leather straps all cut to size. She wants to make a new dildo harness. Mum and Dad have a few technical questions, and Sara shows them the old harness, explains the problems it causes with the dildo's angle or attitude. If only she could afford one of the silicone dildos — they're not floppy, but

flexible, and dishwasher safe. She goes downstairs to help herself to Dad's tools.

For many years Sara spoke with as much condescension as pride about her strange teen years. She saw herself as a late initiate to real life. She put things down in order to move further and faster — then missed them and missed them. She no longer, in private, pretends to be other people, but she does do 'scenes' and — in public — performances. 'People think there's something wrong with us,' she had said, and then set out to control what people thought. She concedes her oddness now, so long as you notice the danger and dissent.

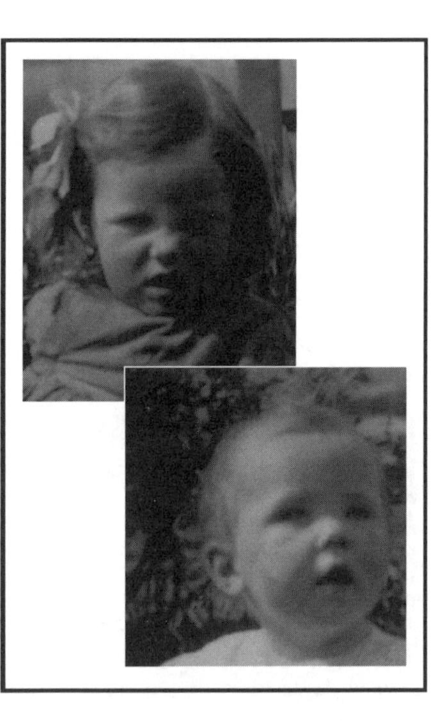

Fiona and Moira Farrell

Phonecalls

Fiona Farrell was born in Oamaru, New Zealand, in 1947. She has published poetry — *Cutting Out* (1987) — short stories — *The Rock Garden* (1989) — plays and a novel — *The Skinny Louie Book* (1992), which won the New Zealand Book Award for fiction in 1993. In 1995 she held the Katherine Mansfield Fellowship in Menton, France. Her second novel — *Six Clever Girls Who Became Famous Women* will be published in 1996. She has two daughters and lives at Otanerito on Banks Peninsula.

Moira Farrell was born in Oamaru in 1949. She produces records, most recently under the Girlzone label. She has two daughters and lives in Boronia on the outskirts of Melbourne.

Fiona Farrell

She rings me at 10 pm.

'Hello,' she says. A warm breathy voice. Mum says we sound identical on the phone and she can't tell us apart. But I think we sound quite different. Her voice is lower, she has a way of giggling while she talks, she has a slight Australian accent. I think my voice is higher and less husky, prissy New Zild.

In our quite different voices, we settle in for a talk at eighty-eight cents a minute, Otanerito to Melbourne. Moira is absolutely relaxed long distance. She makes a cup of coffee while she is talking, lets the dog in, lets the dog out, tells her daughter where the blue pen is. We could be in the same room perched on a couple of kitchen stools. I'm more fretful! My *God, forty* minutes! This'll be costing a *fortune*!

Moira's right to take it easy though. It takes time to get through the 'So, what have you been up to?' phase to get to the point. Because there is always a point.

Our mother, perhaps. Is she all right, down there in Dunedin, in her little house? Eighty-four, with failing eyesight? Are we being neglectful in not persuading her to go into a home as our cousins suggest? (She, who has never yet been persuaded to do a thing she didn't want, who always got her own way though my father yelled and argued, though we squirmed and said 'Oh Mum', trying the full force of our embarrassment.) Moira comes over to visit as often as she can but it's difficult, she and her husband run

a busy recording studio in Fitzroy, she has two daughters who are still at school, she has three horses, two dogs and a cat to care for. I visit Dunedin maybe twice a year; I've been juggling jobs and writing and two daughters. It's not easy to get away.

We reassure one another: Mum's okay. She's phoned, she sounded happy. She's still walking into town every day to the library and the Senior Citizens' Club for lunch. She's been off on a bus tour to Southland. She had a giddy spell a couple of weeks ago but she's gardening again. I tell Moira that Mum is fretting because I am going to France for the winter: there's a war 'over there'. It could be dangerous.

We laugh as we always laughed at her anxieties. 'Oh Mum! We'll be fine,' we've said for years and years.

We'll be fine hitch-hiking. *Tons* of people do it.

We'll be fine in London.

We'll be fine driving down at Easter.

Stop fussing . . .

We laugh and squirm as she articulates with absolute accuracy our inner fears, tells us the world is not to be trusted. She has been around since 1910 and she knows that wars can happen 'over there', beginning in some insignificant village. She knows that Harrod's can be bombed, that that girl (what was her name now?) was raped and murdered hitching from Timaru.

'I keep telling her the war's in Bosnia, miles away from France, but she won't listen,' I say, and Moira laughs. Mum won't even visit her in Melbourne, she says. Melbourne, too, is 'over there'. You have to fly to get over there, entrusting yourself to the mysteries of aeronautical engineering. 'Oh Mum!' we say. 'Flying's quite safe. It's safer than walking across the Octagon.' (But then there's Lockerbie. There's Erebus. There's the plane with the hole in the fuselage and the people sucked into the engine, that young woman with her long hair streaming in the wind . . .)

'I'd really like her to come and visit,' says Moira. And I say she won't, she wants us to visit her, to come onto her territory.

When we visit her we are her daughters once more. We may have left home years before, off in our duffel coats to university and on to see the world. We may have spent the last twenty-five years playing being grown-ups. Moira may have been commissioning musicians or developing a new market, I may have been presuming to teach other people, but as we cross that threshold we are thirteen again. Mum looks us up and down.

'Do you want me to iron your shirt?' she says. (Just the collar and cuffs, Mum. It won't show under my uniform.)

'Have you been eating properly?' (Yes. I've even cooked it myself.)

Or that clincher: 'Is that what they're wearing these days?' (Linen jacket, shirt and Italian shoes all one with the suede mini, knee-high boots and coloured tights that marked the break with tartan skirts and woollen jumpers back in 1964. Moira has ironed her hair straight and I've curled my page-boy.)

We stand at the door, forty-seven and forty-five, and sigh.

'We're fine,' we say. 'The shirt's fine.'

Though you're never quite sure, are you? The jacket might be a tad too long and the shoulder pads might be a tad too large, and the shoes might have been too expensive really and they're not all that comfortable. And the shirt probably does need ironing.

We joke about it on the phone as we joke about the good advice: how we never admit to so much as a cold because to do so invites the litany: a nice blackcurrant drink, just a spoonful of jam and hot water, or a hot toddy, lemon juice, honey, hot water and a wee shot of medicinal whisky, and are you wrapping up warm? You're not overdoing it, are you? You always overdo things and that's when you get run down and come down with a cold. At the first sign of a sore throat you should gargle. Hot water and a whole dessertspoonful of salt and that takes care of it . . .

And of course we probably *are* overdoing it, and we *have* got run down. And it would be so nice, wouldn't it, to climb into bed with some dress-up dolls to play with, and a comic because reading small print strains the eyes, and a glass of hot blackcurrant drink on the bedside table. And Mum doing what she was trained to do and is good at: nursing people and taking care of them.

And healing us, because back then there didn't seem to be anything — measles, mumps, chickenpox, even scarlet fever — that could not be cured by lying in bed and sipping blackcurrant drink.

We don't admit to the illnesses of adulthood and we laugh about the good advice, while we pass it on to our own daughters. Peel apples because of the sprays, eat a green leafy vegetable every day, don't speed when you're driving, be careful on the roads. Sensible words, worn smooth with so much saying.

Moira and I laugh and it's a special kind of laughter, the kind that can easily slip into tears. I don't laugh like that with anyone else. When we were little, we used to have Giggle Nights. We'd jump up and down on our beds, she on her bed with the Snow White stickers on the wall, me on mine with Cinderella. (I'd have preferred Snow White but that was the way it was: my father had put his hands behind his back and we'd had to choose blind.) We'd jump up and down on the saggy wire wove and laugh and laugh until we were almost in tears.

There's still something of the Giggle Night when we talk on the phone, when we talk about our mother, and our father who died ten years ago after being ill for over thirty years, miserably crippled with arthritis. We talk about our own children. Her two daughters and my two daughters. (We favour symmetry in our family.) About our work. About our marriages. About miscarriages and falling in and out of love, about hot flushes and horses and money and anxieties I'd confess to no one else.

We're sisters. There are almost exactly two years between us. I was born on 1 October 1947, she was born on 21 October 1949. Our birthdays fell hard on one another's heels. My birth I always understood to have been a happy one. Moira's was after a troubled pregnancy and when she was born my mother spent some time in a Karitane hospital recovering while I went and stayed with my Auntie Jessie. I

have a peculiar and vague memory of a high room which I think may have been my mother's room at the hospital but I'm not sure. Anyway, Moira was always more delicate than me. She was the pretty one, with naturally curly hair and brilliant blue eyes. 'Farrell eyes' inherited from my father. I was generally described as 'sturdy'. I had straight hair that I wore in stubby plaits, and I had freckles. 'Falconer freckles' and 'Falconer hair' inherited from my mother's side of the family. I was the serious one.

We've talked about this on the phone too: the way those definitions of self have shaped us. Why, as a result, I always felt plain while she felt stupid. It wasn't even true. She was — and is — clever and I wasn't exactly Quasimodo. But that was the way it was. As a result, when we were teenagers she hung out with surfies, while I stayed sedately with my friends from school. She had a scarlet woollen minidress and a suede miniskirt and a two-piece bathing suit. I favoured a navy skirt and a white blouse, a kind of discreet uniform. She dyed her hair blonde, then jet black. I stopped at a smidge of Maybelline blue on the eyelids.

We both went to university since neither of my parents had had the chance during the Depression and that was expected, and we both had teaching studentships since that was the only way we could afford to go. Then she lived with a surfer and drove an ancient but wonderfully speedy red MG and owned an Irish wolfhound. Then she moved to England and met a bass guitarist from Melbourne and married him and opened up a recording studio back in Fitzroy. I married a Commonwealth Scholar and went to live in Oxford and then Toronto where I did an M.Phil. in drama, then home to a part-time lectureship at Palmerston North Teachers' College. I drove a mini, then an Austin Princess. I owned bantams.

There was always, I think, a kind of uneasy competition between us based on the recognition that this distinction was unfair, but it has taken us until middle age to recognise and question it.

Moira was delicate and shy. When we visited my aunties I would willingly sing for the assembled adults in the sitting room. *Peggy O'Neil. Whispering Hope. The Rose of Tralee.* No worries. I wanted adult attention and preferably applause. I was going to be an actress like the girls in Noel Streatfield. Moira refused to perform. When we quarrelled late at night in our adjoining beds, I yelled and flung books. She went quiet. She told me recently that she had figured out early on that this was by far the most irritating response she could make. She also told me she had figured out the ice cream deception. I was a biter, she was a licker. I scoffed my ice cream in big bites then said it must have been smaller. The quicker the finish, the smaller the cone. Therefore, QED, I was entitled, out of fairness, to a bite of hers as well. She always handed it over and I thought I had her fooled, but she said she had given in simply because it wasn't worth the fight.

Despite the shyness, Moira was by far the braver rider. We owned a pony, a skewbald ex-rodeo number called Jaffles who we discovered, a day or so after we had bought him from a crooked little Southland farmer, could buck like nothing on earth. I fell off every time, in a sickening slow-motion slide as

he leapt and twisted and heaved beneath me. Moira was smaller but she hung on. And not only did she hang on, she finally got onto him with a stick torn from the hedge and she clung on bashing him till he stopped bucking and he never tried it with her again. She was — and is — a born horsewoman, a natural. She took after our grandmother, my mother said, who used to ride from Dunedin to Elderslie in North Otago with her best clothes tied to the saddle for parties and horseracing and dances.

We rode past the ruins of Elderslie often on our Saturday expeditions. Moira rode Jaffles and I rode a sort of borrowed sofa-on-legs called Darkie, who ate his head off, could barely be persuaded to trot and who suited my timid temperament just fine. At A & P shows, Moira also rode a pony called Tiny Tim, collecting swags of ribbons which she hung above her bed beneath the Snow White stickers. I never won a single ribbon and Darkie and I came bottom in the dressage at the Pony Club One-Day Event.

The ponies gave us freedom. We rode all over North Otago and twice on our own all the way to Dunedin, across the Horse Range, along those endless white gravel roads through a sculpted limestone landscape. I loved that: loved being with Moira ambling gently along, stopping to take the ponies swimming or to eat our sandwiches on a hillside in the sun.

We shared the riding, as we shared a loathing for curry, and gaps between our front teeth, and measles, mumps and scarlet fever. No one else got scarlet fever but we did, lying for days and weeks side by side in our twin beds and getting up finally to discover that it was spring and that we had missed our birthdays. I remember that first day out of bed for pavlova-for-tea and a *Tiger Tim Annual* each. Moira remembers being carried outside by my father and the scent of flowering currant by the dunny.

We were dressed alike, both in tartan skirts and homeknitted jumpers, or in coats with velvet collars for best. We were both half-Irish/half-Scots, half-Catholic/half-Presbyterian and though people might not have been aware of it, we were both pretty noble. On my father's side we were the descendants of Niall of the Red Hand and the Kings of Ireland. On my mother's side there were the Early Settlers who had their photographs in the Pioneer Gallery in Dunedin. So just between you and me we had the edge on those in Oamaru who were merely wealthy. We may have lived in an elderly and distinctly unfashionable villa, we may not have owned a car till I was ten, but stucco-and-brick and the two-car garage were vulgar and flashy and we had the breeding.

When I think about it, our shared childhood surfaces as black and white snapshots. There's us on the bike with Dad riding out to Weston to visit his sister on a Sunday afternoon. I'm on the bar and Moira has the seat on the carrier. It's warm, Dad is puffing as he pedals up Holme's Hill and the hawthorne hedge is in heavy white bloom. There's us in our hut in the ribbonwood chucking stones at the Williamses from up the road. There's us in fancy dress for the school parade. I'm a bride in my cousin's First Communion outfit and Moira is a Christmas parcel in crêpe paper. There's us on

the Horse Range road in the sunlight and another darker image, us on an empty road, late at night. My father has taken us out to Weston in the new car, a wonderful scarlet Standard. He has been having a few drinks to celebrate and we are weaving our way back home when he decides to stop at his mate Warrington's for a nightcap. He's gone for ages, so I say to Moira, 'Come on, we'll walk home.' And we set off. When cars pass, we hide in the hedge and we're not found till we are a mile or so away, down by the stockyards at Waiareka. My aunt is white with rage, my father is shaken, and my mother says he was never drunk again.

I left Oamaru when I was eighteen to go to university. My sister followed two years later. In the holidays back in Oamaru we quarrelled and scrapped, impatient at being part of this family, wanting to stop being sisters and daughters, wanting to be our single mysterious selves. I married at twenty and left soon after for England. I was away for eight years, then settled in the North Island with my husband and children and we were a separate family. Moira married her bass guitarist and settled in Melbourne. My mother and father stayed in Oamaru and when my father died, my mother moved to Dunedin.

Over the past thirty years we have seen one another rarely. I visited Moira once when she was living in England and I was living in Canada.

She was working for a recording company and living in a mews flat in Iver with her husband and another of her enormous dogs, an Alsatian.

She showed me their wedding photo. She is standing with Norman on the stairs in the registry office. She is wearing white silk pyjamas and carrying a single lily. I had married in veil and Thai silk because that was what everyone did, in an Anglican church with bridesmaids and a reception in the Gold Room because that was what everyone did. My dress was an uncomfortable sheath with a high Victorian neck and an irritating train.

Moira always had more style.

I had taken my eldest daughter Susannah to England with me. We all went blackberrying and we went to Windsor for an afternoon. Moira and I felt like strangers. We had one day when I was deliberately annoying and she was silent. But we cried when we said goodbye at Heathrow.

The next time we saw one another was at my father's funeral. Too many people kept bringing too many sweet cakes to the house in Oamaru. When we visited my father at the undertaker's, he was dressed in a monk's habit. We didn't recognise him. On the day of the funeral we fled the afternoon tea and went down town where we walked up and down Thames Street past Cagney's Booksellers and Woolworths and Hallensteins, trying on clothes at every dress shop. Neither of us bought a thing.

Two years later Moira visited me in Palmerston North. My mother came too but she refused to stay with us and insisted on driving back to a motel she had booked in Lower Hutt.

'Oh Mum!' we said, but she was determined. She said she'd feel more comfortable there.

In 1991 I visited Moira in Melbourne. We hurtled up into the Dandenongs to see her daughters' ponies. They are both good horsewomen too. Then we drove back into the city,

roaring along in her Landcruiser, racing a thunderstorm. She had my father's chair in the living room and some of his books. I visited the recording studio and we walked down Brunswick Street and had Japanese food at her favourite restaurant. My marriage was ungluing while I was there. She and I lay by the swimming pool in her back yard and a kookaburra was laughing hahaha in an old gum tree, there was the possibility of snakes in the dry brown grass, and her dog — another Alsatian — kept chasing his tail. Our daughters plopped in and out of the pool and splashed one another. We had one day when I was annoying and she was silent.

'What's going on?' said our daughters. 'Why are you two fighting?'

That night we all went into town and had hamburgers and all the younger sisters said all the older sisters were too bossy.

We talk about such things on the phone. We compare notes, detect patterns. Moira says her older daughter is methodical and organised, like Mum. I say neither of my daughters is noticeably methodical but the younger one is into music and clothes, like Moira. 'She's got four earrings in each ear and a nose stud and now her hair is dreaded,' I say.

And Moira says her younger daughter is the same, only she also has black nail polish, plays the bass guitar and is forming a band.

At eighty-eight cents a minute trans-Tasman we circle endlessly back to the past and forward in great loops and tangles while the coffee cools and the dog scratches to be let in and our partners go off to bed.

Somehow she and I have ended up in opposite corners. She the country girl, who loves being on her own with her cats and dogs and horses, who gets up at 5.20 a.m. to feed them all before work, has ended up living in a city. She lives on its outer edge but it is nevertheless a city. She makes records. She has her own label, Girlzone, which is the biggest (she giggles and says because it's the *only*) recording studio and distributor of women's music in Australia. She sends me the CDs for Christmas: Jane McCracken, the Snapdragons. And she tells me about it when she phones. She tells me about the fights with DJs who won't pay attention to new bands, let alone Melbourne bands, let alone women's bands. She tells me about their first CD being voted album of the week on Kim Wilson's *Video Smash Hits*. She tells me, too, about her acting, because each week my sister, the girl who hid behind the piano rather than sing for her aunties, plays the woman-in-the-coffee-shop and the hotel-receptionist and the (speechless) prosecuting-attorney on an assortment of television soaps. I look out for her in the crowd scenes.

And me, the townie, I'm living at the end of a gravel road, an hour and a half from movies and plays and a decent vindaloo.

We're happy in our corners but it's a surprising turn of events, not at all what we might have expected.

'Well,' she says from her corner, 'it's getting late.'

'And this call will be costing you a fortune,' I say from mine.

And we hang up having said all we want to say to one another, for now, and feeling better for having said it.

Thank you, Alexander Graham Bell

Moira Farrell

We're sitting on the grass in our backyard, splitting open peapods and eating the peas one by one. Two little girls, side by side, shoulders hunched over, hand-knitted cardigans, pleated skirts, legs stuck straight out in front, grass-stained knees, grey wrinkly socks, scuffed brown leather shoes. Fidgeting, leaning against each other, soft little-girl murmurs, damp sniggers through our noses as we latch onto some idea and try to have the last word, until one of us says something so silly the other collapses in giggles.

The sky is clear New Zealand blue with white gulls swooping and watching us and, like us, they're never still and never silent. The wind from the Pacific is salty and fresh and we can hear the waves down on the foreshore.

They're never still or silent either.

At night the girls run up and down the full length of the hallway, pink and warm after a bath, running bare-bottomed from the steamy bathroom to bang on the strong front door. The brass number on the outside is a magical double dose of fives.

In winter when it gets really frosty the girls have their bath in a tin tub in front of the fire. Afterwards Mum tells them stories about when she was young and lived on her farm. The story about her two pomeranians who disappeared after she left home to go and train to be a nurse. (That was a sad one.) The one about Te Kooti, their horse who was a cross between

Lassie and Moses. Or Dad reads to them. *The Famous Five* were probably our favourites complete with such classic lines as 'Timmy the dog jumped up, barked, ran across the room, up the wall, across the ceiling and down the other side.' Fiona always saw through that one but in my mind I saw a big hairy dog doing exactly that.

Then the girls go to bed. Cinderella tells her story around the top of Fiona's bed and every night Snow White tells hers around me. When we got older Mum wallpapered the room and covered up the friezes but I knew they were still there under the blue flowery paper. I never thought I'd lose them altogether.

On another afternoon we're sitting with the Williamses, the Russells and the Johnstons in a row along the fence by the letterbox recovering from bike races around the block. The fence is white limestone blocks and Dad built it. It's part of the house looking its best when we come whizzing round the corner out of Arun Street and into Greta Street to find it tucked into the dip on the street, sitting pretty in cherry blossom and painted lacework. We bike down the drive past the Scotch thistle, which refuses to forget about it all and die despite Miss Gibson next door, who spends much of her life planning its murder with massive doses of salt and boiling water poured over the roots. It simply grows bigger and stronger than ever.

And on the other side there's the ribbonwood with its cave under the branches and the white flowers in spring and all the other smells just lining up to be breathed in as we walk around the house at lunchtime with fresh bread hollowed out

so that only the crust is left: daffodils, snowbells, peony roses. When we were ill with scarlet fever we stayed in bed for weeks with the blinds drawn for our eyes. We went to bed in winter and got up in the spring in time for our birthday tea. Dad carried me outside and all I could smell were the pink flowers on the tree by the toilet.

Then I'm sitting in the quadrangle at high school. The buildings surrounding me are tall and grey stone and very Scottish. There are hundreds of grey-clad girls moving around talking, talking, talking. The in-crowd keep to themselves and shriek and yell as they get together right in the middle of it all. Pammy Armstrong and I sit on the benches by the wall and munch our horrible sandwiches and watch them, fascinated by their confidence and the way their bodies move toward each other as they touch and toss their hair back. Their eyes widen and their cheeks grow red. Please God, for Christmas can I have a proper plastic lunchbox with a cordial drink and a home-made cake, instead of jam sandwiches on three-day old bread, squashed in a brown paper bag.

The noise level rises as they all finish eating and get down to some serious talking about the strange and wonderful world of Boys' High School down the road. Pammy and I get up to go to the toilets. We have to walk slowly because Pammy has juvenile arthritis and her legs aren't made for speed. We move cautiously over the fingers and legs of the groups of friends sitting and lounging around.

Then, there they are, right in front of us, that small select group, the *crème de la crème* of the fifth form, gathered quietly by the door. Within every form there are a few who are apart from the mob, and have true friendships with each other. Friendships which are not based on the rumour that some pimply high school boy has told a friend of a friend that he fancies you. (That's a surefire way to join the in-crowd for a week or two.) The *crème de la crème* are different because they are being groomed to leave this small town and excel in the wide world beyond the boundaries of the Waitaki River and Holme's Hill. No bank-telling for them, no shop-assistanting, no serving meals to sweaty black-singleted freezing workers, not even the noble sacrifice of nursing. They are at the top of the school pyramid.

My sister is there with them, relaxed and happy with her friends.

Sweet, serious, laughing intelligent faces. She is slim, thick auburn hair in plaits, freckles over her nose, blue-grey eyes. She is standing with her back to me, leaning with one scuffed black school shoe up on the bench. Her friend Pat looks up at me as I go by and smiles.

'Hello, Moira.'

Fiona doesn't turn.

One of her group looks at me and asks her, 'Is that your sister?'

Fiona nods.

'She's pretty.'

What's this? Pretty? Am I? Time takes on a new dimension as we go into slow motion, sudden silence, and I freeze in my tracks. Fiona slowly turns to look at me and those blue-grey eyes look right into mine. The faces of her friends look up at

me out of curiosity and it all becomes a dream sequence. I see the split-second change of attitude towards me as Fiona sees me for the first time. It's magic. I see how it must be for her to be six or ten or fourteen years old and told to 'look after your little sister' when you should be left to be just a kid yourself. How it took away so much responsibility from me and put too much onto Fiona.

So this was the beginning of adulthood.

We're in a church. Two camps separated by a sweet-smelling, flower-laden aisle. We are witnessing a strange performance where my sister Fiona is being 'given away' by one man to another. It is really weird. We are both dressed in Victorian-style clothes and my Dad has discarded his tobacco-smelling Harris tweed jacket and Irish greens and browns for a thin black suit that smells of mothballs. It is all strange, and strangest of all is the feeling that we are involved in a theatrical performance which has been played in caves and church theatres since the beginning of time. Weddings are so pagan!

Then we're standing in front of the house in the sun and starting to enjoy the glamour of the silk dresses and our professionally made-up look. We've survived the formalities. I sang too loudly in church from nerves and made Dad embarrassed. He didn't sing at all. Perhaps we should have had an Irish medley just for him, or had the ceremony in the bathroom at home because that's where he really likes to let loose and sing. The windows are open in the never-used front room and Fiona's friends are all just climbing in and out through them to get to the food and drink. We laugh at that and Fiona looks happy and pleased that it's all over. Mum worries that the house is not good enough for the new relations and Dad has a whisky and relaxes at last.

We're living away from home. Fiona is in Canada with her new baby and husband and I'm in England with a new husband, living in a flat outside of London. We haven't seen much of each other and don't talk on the phone. I get progress reports from my mother on Fiona's life. She comes across the Atlantic to stay with us. Her daughter has blue Farrell eyes and wears a little duffel coat. Fiona wants to go out to a play with me and we arrange for my husband to look after the baby, then I decide not to go at the last minute and Fiona goes on her own. The baby cries at being left with strangers and I don't know what to do.

The world is full of strangers. I've married one of them and together we spend thirty-eight hours on a horror Garuda flight with fourteen stopovers and a six-month-old baby to travel to Melbourne. Fiona finds New Zealand again and gets divorced from her stranger.

I don't think either of us really understands the art of marriage.

The phone rings and I answer it.

'Hello,' she says.

Her voice is bright, quick, warm, happy.

'Hello,' I say, when what I mean is, 'Welcome, come in, pull up a kitchen stool and let's really talk.'

We're sitting on the green grass in our backyard, fidgeting, leaning against each other and I can taste the peas.

Cilla McQueen

Synthesis

Cilla McQueen, poet and artist, was born in 1949 in Birmingham, England, and arrived in New Zealand in 1953, where she became a naturalised citizen. Her collections of poetry include *Homing in* (1982), *Anti Gravity* (1984), *Wild Sweets* (1986) and *Benzina* (1988). She has won the New Zealand Book Award for poetry three times, and held a Fulbright Visiting Writer's Fellowship in 1985. In 1988 she went to Berlin on the Goethe Institute Scholarship and in 1990 her *Berlin Diary* was published. Her most recent work is *Crik'ey: New and Selected Poems 1978–1994*. She now lives in Bluff at the southern-most tip of the South Island.

I miss my sisters. I'm four years older than Ali, Ali six years older than Fio. We were born in different countries: I was born in England, Ali in Australia, Fio in New Zealand. These days our meetings are rare since our lives have parted us, but we are still close. Now Ali lives in Bali, Fio in Auckland and I'm in Dunedin. They've helped me to write this.

We're Celtic. Our mother's ancestry is English with strands of Irish and Welsh. Dad was born in Australia. A hundred years before he brought our family to Dunedin, where there's a beach named St Kilda, his great-great-great grandfather brought McQueens from the island of St Kilda in the Outer Hebrides of Scotland to settle in Melbourne. There's a St Kilda there too. I love those places over the sea where the bones of my ancestors lie, but most of all I belong to Aotearoa.

Cilla

The section at Frankton sloped steeply to a gravel beach that was narrow or wide depending on the level of the lake. Up by the road Dad put a black hut with a coal range and a white hut where we slept. He made a stone patio between them. There was schist on the hillside in big slabs, for walls and fireplaces. He planted trees and built a stone retaining wall down the hill from the huts and built the house. The white hut made an extra room. From the terrace you looked down into the lake, so clear you could see all the levels of the shingle stepping down into green. We carried water up the hill. Ali and I played horses astride long manuka sticks. My

horse was called Cracker and hers was Silver. There was a long-drop toilet with a manuka brush fence. Tiny red moneyspiders running over the hot stones in the sun. Lizards. Up the hill there was a frogpond full of reeds where we got tadpoles. On the beach at night we lit fires and caught eels under brilliant Central Otago stars. Mountains, snow, rock, tussock, willows, the breathing lake.

Ali

I remember how the air and water were different there. As soon as you got out of the car you could feel that crisp dryness. It was very invigorating. After a few days there you felt cleaner and clearer. The hills across from the lake from the house were like sleeping lions — tawny and furry in the hot sun. We seemed to know them personally. Each had its own character, and looking around the skyline, we could name most of them.

Fio

I love the hugeness of the mountains. To me they're great beings. I love to be in their presence.

Ali walks slowly, head slightly bent, her long auburn hair swinging forward. The henna gives it golden sparkles. Her slim figure has a natural grace. Her voice is musical. Sometimes there's a hesitancy in her way of talking that seems to betray diffidence, but she's actually steel underneath, my sister. She goes ahead and does what she wants to do, listening politely to the trepidations of other people but not allowing their fears for her to undermine her confidence.

Fio

I was eight. We were at Frankton and Cilla arrived after a trip away. She was seventeen. I was in the hut and she came in to look at her paintings of red and orange flames and blue smoke swirls. She told me she'd fallen in love with Ross. She said I'd love him too. I thought, 'Oh yeah, why should I?', but I didn't say it.

Ali

I remember Cilla reading me *Timpetill* when I was sick, aged five or six. Cilla cutting the hair off my doll when we were in England when I was four. She and I had matching winter coats with velvet collars, and berets. Hers was a magenta crimson colour and mine was blue.

Cilla

Ali had long fair hair and blue eyes and I had short brown hair and blue eyes and glasses. I was mean to her sometimes.

Ali

Fio at eighteen months wearing a corduroy jumpsuit when we were skiing at Coronet Peak. Watching a skater in a blue suit, at Mount Cook I think. I was two or three. Breaking my arm when I fell off a football I was trying to balance on, and screaming as someone carried me up the path.

Fio

I was five. Ali was playing with Margaret next door and I was tagging along. They didn't want me. They were thirteen. I

followed them over to Margaret's place and they told me I couldn't come inside. They were so mean I had a tantrum standing on the path. I screamed and screamed because I was so pissed off and it was so unfair. Then, to my astonishment, Mum turned up looking very agitated. She was cross with *me*, which seemed surprising.

Ali

When Mum was in hospital Dad painted the chest of drawers in their bedroom white and put gold handles on it. It looked quite luxurious. I had a fantasy picture of Mum and Fio coming home from the hospital wearing pink ballet tutus.

Cilla

The day Fio was born we were helping Dad to pull down the old henhouse at Number 5. When Mum and the baby came home from hospital Ali and I decided to make a special red and green jelly. We put the red jelly in the bowl first and let it set, then the green one on top. It looked rather brown. We wanted to turn it out but it wouldn't come out of the bowl so I held it under the hot tap for a minute upside down. It all came out into the sink and we had to gather it up in our hands. Dad made a pavlova, which had to be chipped off the oven tray with a hammer. I remember the Johnson's Baby Powder smell of my baby sister.

Fio

I didn't see much of Cilla or Bugs during my young childhood as they were so much older and they'd pretty well left home. They were vaguely godlike.

Fio's a doctor. She's just arrived from Auckland on the plane. She takes off her shoes. 'It'll take me a while to slow down.' We sit on the deck of my ramshackle house and look at the sea. It's very different from Auckland. Here the clock-time of cities is of little importance. The rhythms of tides and weather, sun and moon rule my days. I have little money and no job except my writing, but I won't starve here. I spin the fleeces I'm given, knit jerseys for my whānau, all day mulling over words that now and again crystallise into poetry in my mind. It's a beachcombing sort of writing, of found and given elements, arising from this place and this life that I lead here. My only problem as a writer, if it is a problem, is that I no longer have much urge to publish it.

Ali

Cilla had Muriel, a very elegant doll with long limbs. I had Jemina, who had various changes of hair. Later, I had Black Dolly, who also had an African name after I had read a story about an African child. Later Fio had New Dolly. They periodically had to go to the dolls' hospital for new hair and eyelashes.

Cilla

My first was Felicity. She had washed-out blue eyes that turned around inside her head. I poked my finger in the socket. She was hard plastic but a cuddly shape.

Cilla

Ali as a teenager ironing her long blonde hair and flattening her fringe with Sellotape. She and Pru led a sophisticated

social life. She used to get out of her bedroom window at night and go off to parties when she was still at school. As the eldest daughter I'd been more restricted.

Fio

I hated and admired Ali. She was the quintessential teenager, constantly on the phone in that little sort of booth between two doors in the hall. She'd lie across the floor with her legs halfway up the wall, crossed, in tight pale blue trousers. She also spent a lot of time in the bathroom and had quite bad acne. One day when I was young I went into the bathroom and she was on the loo. She said, 'Ugh, look at all this blood,' and showed me the toilet paper. I was totally shocked, but impressed. She had posters of Marianne Faithfull, Audrey Hepburn and the Beatles on her walls.

The tide is out and pools remain where baby flounder swim. Beneath the sand is the cockle nursery. We take the bucket to the edge of the channel and do the twist with our feet to find the cockles with our toes, then squat down and dig them with our hands. Oystercatchers and gulls wheel and rest close by. We look across a rippling silver sheet to Aramoana and the harbour mouth, to inland mountains beyond the pale blue coastal hills. I live among seals and yellow-eyed penguins, dolphins, albatrosses, shags, terns, gulls. Once two pure white kōtuku stopped to feed at half-tide just in front of the house, and once an elephant seal lumbered up the beach and across the road and lay for a few days beside Moana's gate. Last week there was a whale in the channel — a shiny hump, a fluke, and gone.

Ali

I wanted to go to Columba in the first place because of the uniform. Margaret was going to go there and she showed me a brochure with a photo of the uniform modelled by the head girl. She was so svelte and elegant. We wore a tailored green jacket with a kilt of Hunting MacKinnon tartan. Hunting Macaroni. A green hat with the silver Columba badge on the hatband. Gloves and sensible brown shoes. Hair off the collar or tied with a green bow.

Cilla

Green bloomers. There were occasional inspections to see that we were wearing the regulation underwear. We preferred scarlet witches' britches. It was difficult to keep the beehive hairdo bouffant under that hat. The kilt was supposed to touch the floor when you were kneeling.

Ali

We'd buy really long jerseys and hitch our kilts up to make them minis. We pummelled our hats into new trendy shapes and stuck them on the back of our heads. When Fio started in the primary school she wore a cotton pinafore of the same tartan in summer, and her wee winter kilt was held up by braces because she had no waist. The kilt pin looked huge on this miniature version.

Cilla

Mum taught French at Columba for many years. She was a gifted and beloved teacher. Languages were my best subject

so I carried on with them at university and became a language teacher too. I wasn't taught how to be a teacher — it came naturally. I just did the same as my mother.

Ali

The garden at Number 23 is where Mum created her own little bit of England in New Zealand. I remember Fio at the age of three or four, going around the garden with Mum and reeling off the botanical names of all the flowers.

Fio

Frankton. I must have been a toddler. I was sitting on one of the big stepping stones made of schist that Dad had used to make a path between the black hut and its terrifying curtain, home to enormous spiders, which I never went near if possible, and the white hut. This is before the house was built. It was lovely sitting on this stone because it was very sunny and the stone was warm. It was also silvery with little red spiders running everywhere, and some very soft blades of grass growing up beside it. I brushed them with my hand to see what they felt like.

Ali

Those family skiing expeditions were a bit gruesome. Car fumes that made me sick, snow and slush, the cold, the awkward and downright painful equipment. Dreadful gadgets like the nutcracker you had to try and get on the tow-rope to go over the pulleys or your fingers would get cut off. But I loved the landscape, the pristine snow in the morning, the mountains marching away into the distance, that blue sky.

Cilla

Held in someone's arms and seeing snow falling, and thinking, 'Wow! This is it!' That must have been before I was six months old, because then we went to Brisbane and there wasn't any snow there. Another is lying in my cot and having a shit, and putting my hand into my nappies and feeling it. It felt sandy. I knew it was sandy because we had been to the beach and I had eaten sand on my ham and tomato sandwich. The interesting thing about that memory is that it's spatial. I can remember the direction my bed was lying: east–west. That was in Brisbane. And the kangaroo that Dad brought home after its mother had been killed on the road. It lived in the chicken-run with the bantams. I used to feed it and look into its big dark eyes, where I was taught to understand the desert. When it grew too big it was taken to the zoo. We went to visit it once but I didn't know which one it was.

We walk out past toetoe and lupins onto the sand. It's early afternoon, sunny, and the tide is full, the shoreline littered with shells, nobody about. I'm so laid back, I think to myself, she must find me really slow. She has brought a breath of the city with her — her steps are brisk, she's alert and energetic. In Auckland she's busy with work, research, marriage, family. Her dark curly hair springs up into the breeze that's refreshing as we walk along. There's a decade between us. Her skin is finer and her hair's still dark. Her hands are smooth while mine are roughened by washing and weather. It's a tougher life here than in town, physically at least. The

beach is on the eastern side of the harbour heads and exposed to north and north-west winds but sheltered from the worst of the southerly. The Flounder Inn is full of gaps and cracks and gets pretty chilly in winter. In summer it's hot and the rainwater supplies run low. Built on the sand, the house is dilapidated and the floors are wonky, but for me it's just right. Before I moved here from town I had a dream called 'Don't Take Your Bag to the Beach', which was about leaving material things behind in order to move somewhere new. I seem to have reverted a few generations to my St Kildan ancestry in moving away from the comforts of the city to a sparer, simpler existence on the edge of the sea.

Fio

At Number 23 when Ali and I slept in the little bedrooms downstairs we used to get up very early on a Sunday morning. I'd creep into Ali's room and we'd get quietly out of her window and go across to Janet's place. We'd all sit up the back of Janet's garden in our dressing gowns and listen to the *Sunday Request Session*. It was incredibly exciting.

Cilla

I was four in 1953 when we crossed the Tasman on a Sunderland flying boat. The water splashed up against the portholes as we landed. On my fifth birthday I sat on our verandah in Dunedin enjoying the aptness of the phrase 'not a cloud in the sky'. About that time I pulled out Mr Piper's seedlings. He had them in a seed tray just over the back fence. They made a satisfying little 'plick' as I pulled them all out. I didn't bargain for Mr Piper's reaction. He came rushing out shouting and I ran away and hid.

Fio

Sometimes at Frankton I would sneak away to a little clearing below the house and lie in the sun listening to the black seed pods of the broom cracking open.

Ali

Playing in a tree that had a loose bough that we used to manoeuvre as if it were the dentist's drill at the Arthur Street School dental clinic that we called the Murder House.

Fio

Going with Mum to the Arthur Barnett's tearooms for afternoon tea. There was a mural at one end. One of the buildings in the foreground had a peculiar black metal structure on top that looked like a gigantic black spider. I'd gaze at it intensely, willing it to jump out of the wall. We'd chat, playing ladies. I had orange cordial and fairy cake.

Cilla

Janet and John. The girl who had ringworm and wore a knitted cap because her hair was all shaved off. Penny down, tuppence up on the trolley-bus. Our phone number was 85180. My best friend Belinda had curly blonde hair. I took Mum's lipstick to school and we put it on and rubbed it off. It was harder to get off than I'd expected.

Ali

Can I cross your golden river? Only if you're wearing the colour blue.

Fio

Ali told me once that Paul McCartney had saved her from a big spider because his poster rustled and woke her up. She was allowed to go to the Beatles concert when they came to Dunedin. I was deemed too young, to my annoyance. She got a Beatles pendant that was really neat and I was jealous. I made a fuss and got one too but it wasn't as good as hers. I used to be dressed up in a pleated skirt with a white top attached, and bobby socks with lumpy wool in them. Ali and Margaret were big Beatles fans but Ali later preferred the Rolling Stones, which was very risqué.

Ali

Obsessed with boys, my skin, hair, friends, clothes — doing the absolute minimum at school. I was faithful to the Beatles to the point of naming a bird I rescued from a cat PRGJ, pronounced Pridge, standing for Paul, Ringo, George, John. In fact I wasn't allowed to go to the Beatles concert, which was when I was about twelve, but I did see Herman's Hermits a year or so later and stood on the seats at the back of the town hall and screamed because it was the thing to do and it was such fun.

I find myself wishing that she'd stay here and have the baby, not go back to Bali. She could live in one of the cribs close by and do her potting. But of course I've forgotten that she has whānau of her own in Bali now, a whole life that I don't know anything about because I haven't visited her there yet. I will before too long, although I get homesick at the thought. I haven't always been so timid. My writing has taken me on many travels and adventures but the work I've written overseas has usually sprung from an intense, almost hallucinatory longing for this familiar part of the world.

Fio

Me at the age of fourteen buying my first sanitary pads. This was in England with Mum and Dad, and my periods had only just started. I remember reading an ad for these pads called Libresse, which looked very pretty in the picture with lots of flowers around them. I found the advertisement comforting but I wasn't all that relaxed about having periods. I went into a chemist in this English country village and nervously asked the man behind the counter whether they had any. And they did! It was incredibly easy and he was very straightforward and nice. He didn't give me any nasty looks that might have said, 'Oh, so you're *bleeding*, are you?' as I suppose I'd been expecting.

Cilla

By the time I was fourteen we had moved to Number 23 in the same street as Number 5. I was just beginning to discover boys. Saturday night socials, boys on one side of the hall and girls on the other. Gypsy Tap, Maxina, Destiny Waltz. I hated having to wear glasses. A boy brought me home one evening in his father's car. This was exciting. I was wearing my angel blouse and a black and white skirt I'd made myself, and a small red ribbon in my backcombed hair. I was so carried away when he kissed me in the garage that I whispered, 'I love you,' just like *West Side Story*. He fled. Coming home

with boys was never much good. I dreaded the clinking of milkbottles that Dad would bring down to the gate just as we were about to attempt a goodnight kiss.

Fio

At Number 23, before the new bit was built on the front, I was walking down the hall calling out to Cilla about something and I went into her room. She and Ross were in a passionate embrace on the bed. I was horribly embarrassed. I backed out fast and went back down the hall to call out, 'Oh it's okay now, don't worry,' pretending I'd never seen them.

Cilla

I got my first period when I was staying at Naseby with Lynn. I had to ask her mother for sanitary pads, which was embarrassing, but she was kind. Naseby is always linked in my mind with Central Otago heat, the colours of clay and tussock, rock, hills, my first blood.

Fio

I wanted to be an astronaut when I grew up but Dad said you had to be attached to NASA and only Americans could be. I was vaguely interested in being a doctor or scientist of some kind. After a while it seemed inevitable that I should be a doctor.

Ali

I wanted to be a secretary or an actress. I'm really sorry Margaret and I were mean to Fio. It was just that we both shared the same passion for the secretarial life and we had to spend a lot of time rehearsing and putting on lipstick and high heels and tight skirts.

Cilla

Trapeze artist, ballet dancer, actress. Something to do with dancing, music, words. I wrote long stories at primary school. The first typewriter I encountered belonged to Helen's mother. I thought it was a great invention. Being a ballet dancer became impossible after an accident in England when my zealous ballet teacher forced my leg into a high arabesque and the injury had to be repaired twenty years later with a spinal fusion. Acting lasted the longest as a passion but teaching took over when I had to earn a living. Then writing came back to me. By then I'd grown up.

Ali

Our family's intense, interesting, stimulating, not quite like other people's families. We were lucky in our parents. They gave us travel, education, leisure.

Cilla

At Number 5 I had a dream about opening the door of the linen cupboard in the hall and a witch came out grinning, saying, 'You lucky hag' in a witchy voice. There were dress-ups in the bottom of the cupboard, a nightie, a silver and white stole, petticoats, scarves, shawls, shoes. A long pink satin dress was my favourite. I used to ask for music for my birthday. I knew *Swan Lake*, the *Nutcracker Suite* and *Giselle*

by heart. I read *Oliver Twist* with delight and anguish when I was eight.

Ali

Number 5. The long hallway that we used to have pots and pans lined up down when it rained. The drawing room where Mum and Dad used to have cocktail parties where everyone used to come for an hour or so and stand talking very loudly — I remember lots of legs — then go off to have dinner. The dining room, which was cosy with the gas fire that had ceramic pillars that looked like fairy castles. There was a bay window in this room where the dining table was. The walk-in pantry in the kitchen where Mum kept Fio's Glaxo. The wind-up rack over the coal range for drying clothes. The precipitous garden with currant bushes, gooseberry bushes and vegetables at the top. A Jonathan apple tree whose apples Dad was very fond of.

Fio

My memories of Number 5 are vague and distorted. Everything was big. Then when I was four we moved to Number 23. Number 23 was an old wooden villa. They pulled down the back part and rebuilt it in the sixties way, low-ceilinged with lots of windows and glass doors. Before the area was lined I was intrigued by the squares of black paper between the wooden squares on the walls.

Cilla

Number 5 was a wooden villa with a green roof and white weatherboards. There was a hallway down the middle of the house with rooms on either side. The kitchen was at the back. It had a cream-and-red kitchen table and chairs and a coal range. Up the back there was a vegetable garden with red and white currant bushes. Daffodils in the grass. A sloping lawn at the side of the house, and behind the house a steep clay bank that collapsed one rainy day and had to be shored up by Dad with a retaining wall. I had pink wallpaper in my bedroom. I used to pop the corners. When I lay in bed at night I'd wait for the familiar thing that happened just before I fell asleep. Things like the door or the wardrobe became extremely large and clear, at the edge of dream. There was a cellar under the house and a large rhododendron tree at the front. We used to climb in it and make necklaces from the dark pink flowers, threading them on strips of cabbage tree leaf.

Te Rauone is an arc of white sand on the eastern side of the harbour mouth between Weller's Rock and Taiaroa Head. It's Māori land and descendants of the old families live here still. Measles wiped out much of the population in the early period of European settlement when the victims took to the water to cool their fever and died of pneumonia. It was the same on St Kilda in the old days when rare visitors from the mainland brought the diseases of civilisation to a population without immunity.

Fio

Dad could be terribly fierce. He made me eat an egg every morning, although I gagged and hated the taste. There was

no need for smacking in our family — the prospect of Dad growling was enough to keep me in line. My hard work at school and probably my doing medicine was to please him. At Frankton he'd slave away building walls or fixing the pump with gritted teeth and blue hands. Most of his tasks involved immense physical work which was part of their attraction. My first boyfriend accused me of hero-worship. It's probably true.

Cilla

There's always been something that reminded me of Dad in the men in my life. He's linked in my mind with the sea because of his stories of being in the navy during the war and because he taught me to sail and love the sea too. His eyes are sea-blue, changeable. He has a wicked fury when it's roused and I recognise that in myself — a deadly accurate and sardonic tongue and a Scots temper. It was Mum who was the calm one, the peacemaker.

Ali

It's difficult to understand men. When you get a glimpse into what motivates them it helps a lot. I don't often like what motivates them.

Fio

I think my attitudes to men were formed by my relationships with Dad and Bugs. I like strong men, preferably as strong or stronger than me. Intelligent men, intense in attitudes to work, love, everything.

Cilla

At home we hardly talked about sex. I still don't find it easy because the words seem supercharged.

Fio

I was introduced to dope when I was fourteen. I was invited to a dinner party at Bugs' flat, where they were all dressed in sort of a mediaeval costume — seventies head psychedelia — and I had a smoke. I got ravingly paranoid and he had to take me aside and reassure me. They were all so much older and more sophisticated than me.

Ali

Sex is so very nice and easy with the right person at the right time and amazingly difficult and unpleasant with the wrong person at the wrong time.

Fio

I tried to be promiscuous once in my twenties but it didn't work because I'm only into sex when I'm in love. I've been aware of my predilection for big shoulders and bald heads for some time. Broad shoulders preferably clad in T-shirt à la Marlon Brando or denim shirts. But it's only relatively recently that I've become aware of my baldness fetish. Quite funny, really. I was looking at one of those ads for men's hair restorer in the paper. To my eye the first picture showed quite an attractive bald man who, in the succeeding pictures, was transformed into a total nerd by the addition of hair. It's not surprising from a psychoanalytic point of view as the important men in my life have broad shoulders and bald heads.

Cilla

I like black leather.

Ali

Most of my intense erotic experiences have an equally intense emotional dimension.

When she left Dunedin she gave me several of her best pots. She understands volume. Her pots are classical in shape and each has its own personality. They are recognisably Ali, to me, beautiful like her. One that I especially like has deer painted around the rim, dark brown against pale grey. She made it after Paul died because she loved the deer at the farm where they had lived together. Bikes were his passion and that was how he died. It was hard for me, being her sister, when she was enveloped by that grief. I could go with her a certain way, but there were acres of it that she had to travel alone, so lonely and desolate. It's the only time I've seen her with short hair. She just hacked it off.

Cilla

We look and think like sisters. I can see both Mum and Dad in all of us. It goes right through our intellects, behaviour patterns, personalities. Ali's blonde and the tallest. Fio and I are smaller, dark haired, the same height and weight.

Ali

I can see the family resemblance in myself. I look like myself.

Fio

I'm about five foot three with curly brown hair that's never done what it's told. There are some grey ones in there but I'm turning them back to brown by spending a lot of time upside down in yogic headstands, which should theoretically increase the blood supply to the scalp — worth a try. My body is small and these days quite strong. I remember standing in front of the mirror when I was a child and thinking, 'That's not me — who is that funny-looking person?' So I subscribe to the reincarnation theory. I'm only now, at the age of thirty-six, becoming properly attuned to the body I've been given this time around.

Cilla

My hair turned almost white overnight when I was thirty-six, after the spinal fusion. Maybe it was also due to the sudden surge of creativity that swept me away around that time. I didn't dye it for a few years and it was interesting to see how people's attitudes towards a woman change when she's lost the colour of her hair, especially elegant female friends, some men, or young women in shops, who make you feel invisible. Then I dyed my hair and became visible again. I like to do these experiments.

Ali

I think all my siblings have beautiful eyes. Cilla's are large and light blue with long lashes, Fio's are large and a darker blue with curlier lashes. Bugs' are deep greyish greeny blue and he has the best eyelashes of all. My eyes are the same colour as

my father's in the sunlight, blue-green. Fio and Cilla aren't as tall as I am and I think this comes from Dad's side of the family. Bugs and I are taller like Mum's family.

Cilla

There's a yin-yang balance between Mum and Dad. Intuition and logic, emotion and rationality, arts and sciences. They're both highly qualified academically. Mum's a teacher and Dad's a doctor. I'm a poet and a teacher, Ali's a potter and a teacher, Fio's a doctor and photographer who loves yoga. Bugs is a mountain-climbing physicist.

Fio

I think my personality is strongly from Dad, perhaps seventy percent. Also assorted body parts. Bandy legs, blue eyes that are not short-sighted, asthma. Facially, I seem to resemble Mum. I get insomnia like Mum. Ability in sciences like Dad.

Cilla

I have no asthma, short sight, Mum's legs. I look like Mum but I recognise Dad's lines on my face. Dad's nose. My personality must be about fifty-fifty Mum and Dad. I can feel them both in me, sometimes more one, sometimes more the other. Ability in languages like Mum.

Ali

Mum's and Dad's genes are spread pretty evenly among us. We're alike and different at the same time in our mannerisms, speech, sense of humour.

Fio

Ali seems more like thirty-thirty Mum and Dad and forty percent something else, perhaps a contribution from an earlier generation. She looks different from me and Cilla. She has a classical sort of face and can be quite beautiful. She's got nice teeth and a lovely smile, but she's defiant about not adjusting her body to satisfy fashion and doesn't shave her legs or wear make-up. Golden brown wavy hair.

Ali

The facets of our personalities reflect our whole heredity and experience.

Ali has brought some pastel drawings with her that she's done in Bali. They show better than photographs the different qualities of colour, of light and shade in the landscape she inhabits there. She's also brought her embroidery to show me, a white tablecloth decorated with fine silken flowers. I show her my own drawings. As I trace the contours of the landscape the outlines sing in my mind at their own pitch and rhythm, weather and light lending them mood and colour.

Cilla

Mum and Dad met and married during the war. Their wedding photograph shows them both in naval uniform. She was a Wren. He was very dashing. She made the difficult choice to live for the rest of her life on the other side of the world, separated from her own family. It must have been very hard to leave them all behind. Her relationship with her

mother and sisters was faithfully maintained all their lives via the blue airmail letters that arrived in our letterbox every four weeks for years and years. Constance is Mum's middle name.

Ali

Living in Bali has made me think a lot about religion, especially about the differences between Hinduism, Buddhism and Christianity. There's a progression both philosophical and historical there. Christianity values the individual and practises compassion. They're both concepts that are a luxury in societies functioning at a subsistence level, where the biggest challenge is survival. Once a society is more affluent, there's more scope for the fulfilment of the individual. I miss Christian values in Bali. It's a society in transition from one based on ancient cultural traditions to a new one in need of principles other than the pursuit of material wealth. The acquisition of status is the driving force of modern Bali.

Cilla

Both Mum and Dad come from long lines of ministers of the church, Anglican on Mum's side and Presbyterian on Dad's. I'm confirmed in both churches, but these days I find my spiritual food in the natural world.

Fio

I've been doing my yoga since David and I split up. It helps with anxiety and improves my self-confidence. I try to do it every day for half an hour or so. I've also become a vegetarian, which is a big step since I used to be a committed carnivore. All of this is a conscious effort to strengthen myself in a spiritual sense, and, if possible, to become more enlightened. I still go to the Anglican church now and again. I get a similar sense of clear calm from there as I do from holding the yoga balance postures. I'd like to achieve higher levels of consciousness and become more tuned into the patterns of the universe, which is really my concept of God. This is one of the strongest influences on my life in general at the moment and it's helping me mentally and physically. Sometimes I slip back to red wine and cigarettes.

When we reach a certain spot towards the other end of the beach Fio stops. 'Shall we go back?' I don't need to ask why. Last time she came we turned back at the same point. The air gets a little colder there, but it's not just that; there's a change in atmosphere, it feels as though it's private, intense, different from the rest of it. We turn and walk back towards the house. We have a sensitivity to the vibrations of place. Some places are more charged than others. Living on this beach I can feel the layers of Māori history beneath the tranquil surface. It has an ancient and secure feeling about it. Across the water from here a cloud still hangs over Aramoana. The tragedy that happened there thickened the air and it hasn't cleared yet.

Cilla

Dreams are important in my waking life. I recognise things I've dreamed, months or years later. They speak in symbol and metaphor and time means nothing to them. They're

emotional and spiritual. House dreams and water dreams help me understand my life. By listening to my dreams I've learned to write poetry.

Ali

I have frequent and recurring house dreams. Usually it's a house that's just been vacated by somebody who has left a lot of things behind, clothes especially. Often the person was an old lady. Sometimes I'm in one part of the house and I can look out of a window at another part of the house that is closed off and inaccessible. Sometimes I will have gone to considerable lengths to lock a door and then, thinking that the house is secure, I'll find another door still wide open. One version was very liberating. I was standing in a room with the windows wide open wearing old-fashioned clothes and throwing other old clothes out the window, shouting, 'Freedom!'

Cilla

We spent a year in England when I was twelve and we lived for part of the time in Evesham in a fifteenth-century farmhouse. It had a closed-off wing. We looked through the back of a cupboard into a dusty stairway. There was the skeleton of a bird on the stairs. That house has been the model for some of my house dreams.

Fio

A water dream that's stayed with me goes like this. I was walking around the outside of the house. It was a brilliantly fine day and the sky was dark blue. The house was dazzlingly white, so bright it almost hurt my eyes, a stucco Mediterranean-style with a flat roof and square walls. I walked down some steps and beside a swimming pool that looked cool and inviting, aqua green with lines on the bottom. I had the feeling I always have in water dreams, that something was going to happen. I was slightly excited and scared. I walked up some steps on my left beside a high white concrete wall, wanting to see what was at the top. As I climbed the feeling of expectation grew stronger until I could see over the wall, and then I knew why. I'd thought there'd be a view over the city but just at the level of the top of the wall, which was quite thin, was the sea. A vast blue ocean at eye-level and rising, just licking at the top of the wall and about to spill over. And when it did, all the tidy house and garden and life and hopes and vanities and conceits would be deluged. Could be to do with sex, but maybe just global warming. I gather the Ross ice shelf is breaking up.

Cilla

A combination house and water dream was of being scooped off the land and washed by a wave over a black rock cliff. As I went over I saw that there was a small window in the rock, with leadlight panes. I went inside the window and found myself in a room with a fire in the grate. Near the window was a polished wooden table and on the table a magnifying glass. It was quiet in the room. Green light filtered in through ferns beyond the panes.

Ali

I had a peculiar dream about a psychically charged cupboard. It was a cupboard under some stairs and it emanated such a strong psychic force that we had to get a priest to exorcise it which he did wearing his priestly robes and chanting appropriate mantras. It reminded me of Cilla's 'Lucky Hag' dream. The best dreams I've had have been vividly coloured ones where I've seen beautiful flowers in great detail close up. I remember in particular a black fuchsia flower. Once I saw some stunningly beautiful rainbow-coloured stones.

Cups of tea. Fio's busy and happy but her life as a mother and a doctor is so full she'd like more time for beaches and music. She works flat out like Dad. I was the same myself when I was living in town, teaching and writing and involved in music and theatre. I think that at certain times in life one has to stretch oneself to the limit and push it further. At other times there's apparent inactivity. The creative energy is still there but working differently, more inwardly, restoring and storing itself.

My writing has changed since I first began. When I first started it all came tumbling out as if a dam had burst. It was all the language and experience that had built up in me until then, of my education, my parents, my heritage.

Fio

I adored Bugs. He was my big brother, immensely tall and wise. I remember seeing him after his bad car accident, when he went through the windscreen on the Portobello Road. Tom was driving and swerved to dodge some cyclists. Bugs sat in his room swathed in bandages from head to foot, looking like an Egyptian mummy.

Cilla

In Brisbane Bugs and I were sitting in the car when a fireball rolled down the road. Another time lightning hit the house and flashed out the plug in the kitchen just as Mum put down the iron. I didn't like tomato soup. Once when Bugs and I were having it for tea I decided to try out the trick of jerking the tablecloth out from under the plates on the table. It didn't work very well and he got tomato soup in his lap. He taught me to play chess and always beat me mercilessly. We talked and talked about the stars and the universe. We still do. He spent hundreds of hours polishing a mirror for a telescope he was making. It seemed a boring pursuit to me. I was impressed with his crystal set. I used to tag along behind him and Max. Sometimes they'd need me in their games but more often not. I liked having an older brother, especially when I first started school.

Ali

When we were growing up Bugs was usually preoccupied with making a telescope or something equally esoteric. I appreciate his scientific interests a lot more in retrospect and I wish I'd had more grounding in them when I was young. But that comes of being labelled the dumb blonde early on.

Our feet are bare, the sand warm. Even when it gets very hot here as it does in summer the air's still dry and there's usually a breeze

off the water. Ali's happy to have a change from the tropical heat but she's determined that the baby should be born in Bali. She knows I've been scheming to keep her here. 'No,' she smiles. 'I have to go home.'

Fio

Bugs' room at Number 23 had a dark blue carpet. He was into astrophysics and the carpet was like the night sky on the floor. I gazed in awe at his radio with all its fascinating glass and shiny bits. I couldn't imagine how he could have built it.

Cilla

It was Bugs who explained to me that Father Christmas didn't exist. I didn't mind. It was nice of Mum and Dad to play the game. We'd put a drink of milk and some cake out for Father Christmas before we went to bed on Christmas Eve and when we woke up the food was gone and there was the weight of a pillowcase on the end of the bed.

Ali

Christmas was pretty manic, with the Christmas tree and presents and laughing and joking. Dad heating brandy in a tablespoon over a candle flame and pouring blue fire over the pudding that Mum had hidden sixpences in. She gave us the traditional English Christmas, although she always seemed puzzled that the weather was hot, the season all wrong.

Cilla

Happy birthdays too. Cheerios and tomato sauce. Hundreds and thousands on white bread. Jelly. Fizz. On my fifth birthday I sat on the front doorstep in the sun. The sky was brilliant blue, not a cloud in it.

Fio

Every year I get a birthday present from fate. Last year it was Harvey asking me to marry him. Another time was a beautiful grasshopper sunning itself on the doorstep. Once it was finding a little green shoot peeking out of the ground near the letterbox. I potted it and it grew into a pinky-orange gladiolus. I love gardening, especially raising little plants from seed, closely watching God's efforts.

Home. This beach is my home. Apart from a couple of years here and there and plenty of travelling in the outside world, my home has always been in Dunedin, where my parents live too.

From halfway up the beach we can see the clay-coloured scar of Port Chalmers. Just to the right of it is Carey's Bay. In the middle of Carey's Bay is the house where I used to live with Ralph. That still feels like home too. I used to sit on the verandah over there writing poetry, looking northwards towards the harbour heads and this beach where we are now walking. Te Rauone catches the sun until late at night in summer, long after the shadow of the hills has fallen on Carey's Bay. In those days one of my favourite occupations was to draw the hills of the peninsula, sometimes from Carey's Bay and sometimes from Aramoana. I drew that landscape a thousand times, and now I am living in it and looking back to where I used to be. My life has taken me around the harbour, from the western side of the heads to the eastern side. I wonder whether my life has produced the

themes of my poetry, or whether it's the other way around and the demands of poetry have dictated not only the spiritual but also the physical direction of my life.

Ali

The lives of my children have been very different from mine. In the case of my sons, their father and I were separated when they were aged six and ten. I don't think this affected them adversely psychologically but it did make our life difficult. As far as my daughters are concerned they have another dimension completely, which is their Balinese ancestry. It's been a great learning process for me, trying to help them integrate their Balinese and European heritages.

Cilla

I see a lot of myself in my daughter, and now and again glimpses of her father. She has two fathers, her birth father whom she knows but hasn't seen much of, and her adoptive father, Ralph, who has given her a Māori heritage that she's fortunate to have. He also gave me a lasting love of Māori language and culture which is flowering again here in my life at Otakou. My daughter has no sisters. I'm sorry about that, but she does have cousins. There's a strong family resemblance among them and they seem like siblings. Mum's very close to her three sisters, who are in their eighties and nineties now, still lively. They all keep closely in touch although they live apart, and their family resemblance is reflected in their handwriting, whose similarities and differences I came to recognise on their blue airmail letters.

Fio

One of my memories of childhood is of loneliness. I was the last in the family, with older parents. I often allow my daughters to have friends over to play with because I remember how much I used to want that as a child. Our upbringing was very stable in that Mum and Dad were always together. But perhaps my girls have a wider perspective.

Ali

Mum and Dad are probably wiser than I'll ever be. Their stability as individuals and as a couple gave all of us and our children a really solid background for our lives.

Cilla

I like the old story of a boatload of St Kildans who went to a neighbouring island to buy grain. Somebody asked them a question and all thirteen of them gave exactly the same answer simultaneously. Our family seems to have that sort of mind-contact.

Ali

Balinese people believe that they are recycled members of their own family. Not just one person but several. The Balinese emphasis on individual similarities rather than differences makes me see how much human life follows a pattern that is repeated over and over again. It's karma.

Fio

We seem more psychically connected to each other than

many families. Sometimes there are great similarities in our thought patterns. One of the ideas I've come across about reincarnation is that bands of souls tend to travel together through their successive lives. It's comforting. Perhaps we're a group and we've known each other before.

Our conversations twine like Celtic knots. Three sisters, three strands, three branches. Same sap, same seed. We're looking north-west from the windows at the front of the house. Across the water are three volcanoes, etched paua blue against the paler sky. The tide recedes, dusk falls, the channel lights shine red and green. Between east and west the water is the membrane, the elemental barrier and communicator. The sea, thoughtwaves, miraculous translations of thought into language, genes into living flesh, seed into tree, all subject to tide and weather and the moods of the earth and sky. Wordless thought flows like water.

Sue McCauley

Elisabeth and Susan

Sue McCauley was born and grew up in Waitahora Valley near Dannevirke, New Zealand, and now lives in Christchurch. She has published four novels: *Other Halves* (New Zealand Book Award and Wattie Book of the Year Award winner 1982), *Then Again* (1986), *Bad Music* (1990) and *A Fancy Man*. In 1986 she was writer in residence at Auckland University and in 1993 at Canterbury University. She has also written short stories, drama for television, film and stage and wrote the script for the film of *Other Halves*. She also works as a script editor and script-writing tutor.

Our current cat sleeps on his back, legs limply spread-eagled. He does it in public places, making me anxious on his behalf. The world, I tell him, is a fierce place. Cover yourself up, be wary. Such manifest trust invites attack. Possibly by me.

Our current cat reminds me of my sister and the way we were. Yet when I tell her I've been asked to write about her she says (predictably) that I'll find little to say, and then relates a handed-down family story of the time when young Elisabeth sat on a bee in her pushchair and, on being stung, wished aloud that she had put her baby sister Susan there instead.

I suspect the story has lasted because it was my sister's only moment of childhood malice. It's not until I sit down to write this piece that I realise how unusual such goodness must be. Without even knowing the word I thought of it as *guilelessness* — an invitation to take advantage.

There was the Mrs Fettes's toothbrush incident. Mrs Fettes, a mild-mannered war widow with a young son, was our father's housekeeper. One night at bedtime my sister inadvertently used the wrong toothbrush, and I was watching. For some time — a matter of days as I remember it — I blackmailed her for various favours. *I'll tell! You used Mrs Fettes's toothbrush!*

Eventually she called my bluff. *Tell then.* I probably did, out of chagrin, and got myself told off. I don't remember.

It should be shame that has kept the incident in my memory for nearly half a century, but in fact the emotion it

brings is still one of amazement that someone's threshold of wrongdoing could extend to a momentary appropriation of another's toothbrush. Amazement coupled with the heady sense of being, at least for the moment, in a position of power over someone bigger, older and decidedly nicer than myself.

It wasn't my worst sibling crime. That was when I bit her so hard that my toothmarks remained scalloped on her arm for an awesome length of time. I remember the sense of shock mingled with pride at my wickedness, and I remember that we were in the woolshed paddock behind the plantation, which was then still young. I have no recollection of why I bit her. Because, like our current cat, she seemed to invite attack? Or because I was genuinely aggrieved?

My sister had two major sins: she believed her three years' advantage entitled her to be in charge, and she read too much and too often — which meant (there being only the two of us) that I had no one to play with.

The last isn't strictly true. There was, for a few years, the housekeeper's son, but he was much younger and — alas — a boy. The only game he cared to play was of his own invention. It was called Bulls, and required the participants to get down on their hands and knees and charge at each other head-on. It may have been a useful preparation for life but it wasn't a great deal of fun.

Whereas the games my sister and I played, when I managed to wrench her away from her books, were marvellous and intricate affairs. My favourite was Native People. (In our defence I should point out that those were unenlightened colonial times.) The game was played in the native bush down by the river that snaked through our father's farm. We were each an extended family of bush-dwellers with complicated lineage and inter-relationships. Within that family we switched characters at will, establishing which one we were before 'being' him or her.

In my mind all but the oldest members of 'my' family had more than a passing physical resemblance to the movie version of *Mowgli.* Native People transported me from my short, tubby, freckled and somewhat isolated reality into a world of physical beauty and sociability.

The extended families we transformed ourselves into lived harmoniously with nature, sleeping on ferns and fashioning utensils out of stone and driftwood. They lived rather less harmoniously with each other. In fact we were extemporising a semi-stone age soap opera — but that thought didn't occur to me until some thirty years later when I was earning much of my living from writing drama.

My 'people', I secretly believed back then, were racier and more interesting than my sister's. But the game was her invention — and her 'people' had all the good names.

Thinking up good names was a gift my sister had. It filled me with envy — an emotion she didn't even seem to be acquainted with. Her most inspired, unforgettable, feat of naming was a blue plaster-of-Paris doorstop rabbit with one ear raised and the other flopped down. She studied it for a time and then said it was Belinda. And immediately I saw that it was. That Belinda was exquisitely right and in fact the only possible name for a plaster-of-Paris doorstop rabbit.

But I, too, had a rabbit — identical to Belinda except it was pink. And my sister had usurped the only name my rabbit could ever answer to. I called my rabbit Belinda the Second. My sister didn't protest. I was aware that, in her shoes, I wouldn't have allowed it.

When I set out to write my first book — I was maybe ten or eleven — I sought my sister's assistance on names. What to call a *really horrible* person? 'Maud,' she said after barely a moment's thought. When my finished book — a very brief Western — was launched upon my family, its literary merit was overlooked in the general hilarity over the swaggering, thieving, moustache-tugging villain — Maud.

The mistake clearly wasn't my sister's fault, but I'm sure I blamed her. Blaming was in my nature. There was the time when, on the way to the native bush, I fell over. 'It was your fault,' I gritted.

She looked at me in genuine amazement. 'Why?'

'You jumped, and the ground shook.'

My sister likes to remind me of that. I suspect she secretly believes it epitomises, on my behalf, a somewhat over-dramatic interpretation of facts. Yet I clearly remember the earth giving — the instant before I fell — an undeniable tremor.

By all logic my sister — the voracious reader with the inventive imagination and a knack for naming — should have been the one of us intent on becoming 'a writer'. She was the one with the aptitude. I was the one with the enlarged ego. Though she did write. In her teenage years she kept a diary which, once, I sneakily read. But only enough of it to shame me with the realisation that this was the private diary of someone who would *never* sneakily read another person's private diary.

I should have wanted to be like my sister, who was kind, unselfish and unassuming. I didn't. To be so unreservedly nice seemed both limiting and risky. I watched her dealing with the adult world — watched in just the way that miners must have watched the sparrows sent into their coalmines — and it confirmed my suspicions. The path of the truly righteous was full of brambles. I watched my sister and saw the advantages of being opaque and devious.

Yet when I tried to wise her up she seemed not to know what I was talking about. We lived side by side but apparently existed in different worlds. Hers, I gathered, was a less complicated and hostile place than mine was. In her world the earth stayed firmly put. (Though once, inexplicably, she saw a judge in full gown and wig ride a motor bike up the unsealed road that ran past our tiny one-roomed country school.)

I warned myself that niceness could impair your vision.

Then my sister did the cruellest thing to me. She went off to boarding school, leaving me alone and unprotected in my dodgy world. No more Native People. No one to play with; the housekeeper and her son had gone and there were no other children living close by.

I missed her terribly. Alone in our bedroom I discovered I was seriously scared of the dark.

She'd left me with the task of exercising her pony, who was as near as a living animal can come to an inanimate

object. Trixie (for once my sister's gift for appropriate names had let her down) was overweight, slothful and petulant. She was the daughter of my pony, a wonderfully hairy and belligerent creature who showed no affection at all for her daughter. This didn't surprise me; Trixie was something that only my sister could have loved.

Intent on not being like my sister, I concentrated on deviousness. Pretending, I realised, didn't need to be confined to games in the bush. I invented a cheerful, thick-skinned, uncomplicated child with a thimble-sized ego — the kind of child that, in my observation, adults liked, the kind who found life easy. I hid behind this child, cunning and safe.

I picked my way unenthusiastically through my sister's books — Victor Hugo, Georgette Heyer, the unending adventures of Biggles. I found and obsessed over a couple of girls' boarding school books — that terrifying, fascinating world of dorms, prep, new bugs, midnight feasts and crushes. My sister had disappeared into this astonishing world and in three years I would follow her.

At intervals she returned, an alien creature with unknown friends and mysterious preoccupations. I was desperate to know what her new life was like — the boarding school books were English, and therefore maybe not applicable. But, even as she described things, I would be aware that it was Lis's version and therefore unlikely to coincide with mine.

One thing I took to heart — could not fail to, it was so dire. I would be unpopular, my sister warned, unless I ate faster. Everyone at boarding school hated slow eaters because they had to wait for them before they could leave the dining room. A slow eater would have to finish the job with a hundred pairs of contemptuous eyes burning silently into her.

I began at once to train as a speed eater. It wasn't easy. I had to learn to eliminate a lot of chewing and to talk less. I had to open my mouth wider and take larger mouthfuls. I had to put aside the pleasure of pushing my food into geometric designs and deliberating over every subtraction.

But, driven by the spectre of those eyes and that terrible word 'unpopular' (my sister, with her tiny ego, surely had no concept of the high stakes that her boarding school books and my own vast ego had placed on 'being popular'), I became a speedy eater.

I ate faster than our parents. I gobbled my food, swallowing it unchewed, my utensils moved at the speed of light. But still I was anxious; how fast was fast enough?

Finally I, too, went to boarding school. My sister was in the sixth form, she had a superior room long corridors away. Her friends were lofty seniors, almost adults, and they knew her much better than I did. To those of us in the new bugs' dorms sixth formers were objects of awe; sisters or not, we didn't fraternise.

I didn't mind too much. I discovered I was a fast eater by *anyone's* standards, and 'being popular' loomed as a possibility. I began to edge out from behind the cheerful, uncomplicated pretender with the thimble-sized ego and be myself for better or worse.

In classes my sister had smoothed a path for me. Her teachers remembered a conscientious, intrinsically nice student and smiled on her sibling. At least until they knew me better.

My sister left school the following year, worked as a nurse aide through the holidays, then entered training college. I was so absorbed by the world of dorm-mates, midnight feasts, prep and crushes that I barely noticed.

My sister got her driver's licence. This meant that in the holidays we could drive to the weekly ping pong evening at the local school. I would sit beside her, watching the fenceposts crawl by. She was surely the world's most defensive driver; a horse could have passed us at a steady trot, birds flew from the grass on the left-hand verge as our cautious tyres approached. And already I could see something of myself in my careful, unassuming sister. It was like a warning; conscientious and self-effacing was not the image I had in mind for myself. I felt immense impatience with my sister. What was wrong with her? How could she want so little from life when I wanted so much?

Lis finished her teacher training and worked at country schools. When we did spend time together she didn't tell me much about her life and I didn't tell her much about mine. Nor did we ask each other personal questions. This seems odd to me now but it didn't at the time; it was just the way we were. If personal information wasn't volunteered it would have been presumptuous to ask for it, and my sister wasn't the type to talk about herself. I, alas, was — but in her presence restrained myself.

I left school with no career in mind. The gulf between my private grandiose but non-specific ambitions and the realities of earning a living seemed unbridgable. For a year I worked as a nurse aide at the hospital where my sister had worked before me. Once again she had smoothed my path — remembering her made the staff well disposed towards me.

I found work as a radio copywriter and was immensely pleased with myself. Among my colleagues I might feel like a gauche country girl but alongside my sensible sister I was now dizzy with sophistication. How could I ever have feared we were alike? She was unadventurous, reliable and decent while I was gaudy and almost worldly. My relief was enormous.

My sister saved up her money and sailed away on an ocean liner. Overseas! It was the conventional thing to do, but I was impressed and a little bit envious. She sent me postcards from various parts of Europe, ethnic jewellery and a writing compendium of hand-tooled, embossed Moroccan leather. I imagined travel changing her into a person of nonchalance and panache, not so much broadening her mind as sharpening up the edges of her personality.

After her travels and itinerant jobs she stayed for a time in London, living in Earl's Court with all the other colonial expatriots. She married one of them, an Australian, and sent a snapshot taken at their wedding breakfast. To get married in a registry office in another country, to a good-looking man, marginally foreign, seemed a promisingly exotic thing to do.

She brought him back to New Zealand. I was expecting transformation; she would be urbane, witty, wilful. But the

woman who came back seemed to be exactly the same person who had gone away. Only married. I was stunned. She had visited exciting places and mixed with exotic people and stayed just Lis. Could this mean that being decent and unassuming was really not as internationally unacceptable as I imagined?

They rented a house, a lovely house, on the Plimmerton beachfront. I was working and living in Wellington and in the weekends I would sometimes catch a train out and stay overnight. They lived quietly, industriously; working, studying, saving money. I thought life was passing them by; they should move into the city where there were movies, pubs, concerts and exciting people like me and my friends. They listened politely and smiled.

I also had plans to travel, thwarted only by my chronic lack of ability to save money. I had a night job, cleaning office blocks. This was against the rules for public servants, and broadcasting was in those days still public service. I never quite got rid of the fear that I would be found out. Nor did I manage to save any money. It came, it went.

My sister and brother-in-law bought a section on the hills above a bay and built a Beazley home. I privately thought the treeless subdivision of quarter-acre lots and boxy houses was a graveyard for the living dead. They had a view, but not a car. They took the train to work and home again. They put up curtains and planted a garden.

I could look at my sister at that time and feel that, apart from our foreshortened legs and regrettable thighs, we were entirely unalike. Shape apart, we had never shared a close resemblance. She looked like our mother's side of the family while I took after our father's side. Her eyes were blue and fully functional, mine were an indeterminate brownish colour and, since my teens, faulty. But short-sightedness could be remedied, unlike my sister's — presumably inherited — disability, which was to have no sense of smell. Sometimes I would try to imagine that, thinking of freshly ground coffee, daphne, old-fashioned roses . . . Other times I'd think, with exasperation, how *typical* of Lis to have a handicap that was so significant yet was invisible, so that she got no credit for it.

Alike or not, we got along. *Getting along* was a family trait about which I was periodically resentful. For some years — perhaps from the time my sister went off to boarding school and I was left to my own company — I had nurtured the conviction that I would some day become a writer of fiction. Increasingly the people I hung out with were also convinced that some day they would become writers of fiction. And it was apparent to us all that flamboyant, monstrous or eccentric families were a material advantage to a would-be novelist.

Our family, our relatives, were a disappointment. Either I didn't even know them or they were, like my sister, hopelessly decent and dismally normal. No use at all as the raw material of fiction; they didn't seek power, or conduct vendettas, or mount campaigns. They didn't even join drama clubs or slag each other off in public. They disliked pomp and ritual and were unimpressed by status. *Easygoing* — that's what it was called back then. Our relations were *easygoing* and what was the use in that?

It took a lot of years, and some close-quarter experience of the kind of extended family I'd imagined I wanted, to make me appreciate the merits of *easygoing*. I've now heard too many people I'm fond of talk of their own interestingly aberrant parents with a kind of fatalistic revulsion. *This is what I have issued from, and what I am bound to become.* While I don't believe that genes are the sole dictators of who or what we are, in middle age I have grown very grateful for the reassurance of *easygoing*.

When I finally left New Zealand it was to join my boyfriend in Australia. We fondly imagined we would save the money to get us further afield, but work was hard to find and when we found it the working conditions were abysmal. Besides, neither of us was thrifty. I turned twenty-one and we got married, for no good reason, in a depressing registry office ceremony in Melbourne. A few months later we fled back to the security of New Zealand. My vision of myself as a jaunty risk-taker was severely battered. And I was pregnant.

My sister and brother-in-law had been trying for a family without success and they had their names down to adopt. In New Plymouth I had a stillborn son and within a few days my sister was handed a daughter. A year later I had a son and so did she.

In Christchurch we bought an old house on a tree-laden section in a leafy street. It looked appealing but, in winter, was desperately cold and the charmingly old-fashioned garden was seething with twitch. My vision of myself as an adventurous, unconventional person shuddered and died.

Up there on the Kapiti Coast they were accumulating children. After two adoptions my sister got pregnant and had four more children. They were planning on a total of five but the last baby turned out to be twins. They liked children; in the process of bringing up their six my sister also fostered babies, one over extended periods of time so that he and his real Mum — and eventually his children — became part of the extended family.

I knew my nephews and nieces only through photos — one official portrait when there were only four of them, and occasional snapshots of toddlers peering from beneath the hoods of swaddling windbreakers. This was the sixties and six children were more than fashion decreed. I, who by now had the requisite two children, was turning into the conservative sister.

Six children and still they had no car. That wasn't in itself unusual, but they lived up a hill, and, besides, were an outdoor family, given to hearty walks and bush trekking. Already their once-barren subdivision had become an established and leafy suburban street, with homes increasing and encroaching. So in the holidays they would assemble on railway platforms or bus depots and travel, with whatever equipment that might entail, to scenic holiday baches for a week or so.

Even though my brother-in-law was ahead of his time in being a domestically willing and capable male, these holidays looked, from the outside, like a form of dogged masochism. At best they seemed, surely, a trifle eccentric?

I liked to think so. One of us ought to be. I imagined them climbing from the train onto an otherwise deserted platform in some semi-ghost town. I imagined my sister and brother-in-law walking to the information office with my nieces and nephews straggling behind and the only moving vehicle in sight — maybe an old Austin truck — stopping to wait till they were safely across, just as if they were so many ducklings.

In the meantime my own life was falling apart. Naturally, I'd chosen to marry a risky man, had passed over *kind and decent* in favour of *interesting and complex.* If I was looking for drama, I got it, but it wasn't the sort I'd had in mind.

Separation. Solo parenting. A new partner who was, by all logic, an even riskier prospect than the one before. The upheaval of moving north . . . It seemed that everyone I knew was appalled or deeply concerned at the path my life was taking; except my sister who was accepting, nonjudgemental. As I had known she would be.

I realised then that she and I did, after all, and in general, see the world in the same way. That is from a low angle, looking up. Little people — the social underdogs, the powerless — in the foreground, through a scramble of petty officials to the rich and powerful at the top. And, viewed from beneath, the movers and shakers are all nostrils, belly-jut and underwear. Not a sight to evoke respect or admiration.

The Beazley house on the hill had grown, creeping out over the back lawn. Because the ceilings were low and the passage narrow it felt to me like the card houses we made as children; an intriguing, yet somehow perilous building with rooms branching off at whim.

It was a house that always felt busy with comings and goings; my brother-in-law worked long hours in the city, my sister had returned to teaching. She juggled work and family, complained about nothing except the occasional idiocies of Education Department bureaucrats. The house seemed always crammed with children — their own and others — cats, dogs, potplants, in-progress handcrafts — rugs, knitting, embroidery, bedspreads . . . The garden was a reflection of the house — colourful, cared for and vaguely chaotic.

They tried living somewhere else — rented out the house and moved to the South Island West Coast. But the life there didn't measure up to the one they'd left behind and they came back home and stayed put.

That security of having a permanent home began to seem to me the most desirable thing in the world. We were moving too often, leaping around the country after work for my unskilled partner. Work and a house — it didn't seem such a lot to ask for, but each time we got it recession and restructuring would whip his job away.

In middle age I began to notice the tricks of genetics. Although they barely knew her, my twin nieces sounded indistinguishable from my daughter. Their brothers had mannerisms I'd imagined were exclusive to my son. Once, watching me feed our cat and dog, my nieces burst out laughing — I was exactly like their mother. How? The way I talked to the animals, the obsession with distributing fairly.

I liked the thought. In middle age I wanted to be like my sister. Wanted to *have been* like my sister, who had always just naturally 'done unto others' and so had a heap of good karma

waiting in store. It was only fair. She who had done nothing but sow good seeds would deservedly reap.

Then, one day in 1989, one of my nephews rang to tell me that his twin sisters had been in a car accident, and one of them, Catherine, was in intensive care with serious spinal injuries. Only it couldn't be as bad as it sounded, I was sure of that, because Lis deserved nothing but good stuff. (So, said Lis, did Catherine, who was kind to everyone.)

It was as bad as it sounded, but could only improve. This happened all the time, doctors being confounded by the human body's extraordinary powers of recovery. Besides doctors often made mistakes, and willpower is stronger than medical science, and miracles maybe do happen . . .

It didn't improve, but the hope took a long time to die. The reality was too terrible to accept. One day an eighteen-year-old girl — sporty, tramping, outdoor type — and her identical twin were on their way to a softball tournament; and the next day, and forever after, the girl was a tetraplegic.

The driver of the car the girls were travelling in had swerved to avoid an oncoming vehicle, his car had rolled. The driver in the oncoming car had crossed the median strip while momentarily attending to the sound system in her car.

My sister and her family coped. What else could they do? Through long months of hospitalisation, physiotherapy, home care, through the coming-to-terms-with and the making-the-best-of-it. In all that time the woman who drove the oncoming car made no approach to either Catherine or her family. My sister found this almost beyond belief. Not even flowers or a note to say she was sorry.

That woman was a doctor of medicine. At the time of the accident she had not left her car to give assistance. That, my sister could just accept — she may well have been in a state of shock — but she couldn't accept the lack of an apology.

Eventually the case came to court. The woman was fined two hundred and fifty dollars for careless driving. She didn't lose her licence, because, as a doctor, she would need it. My niece's loss and future were apparently not considered relevant. To my sister it seemed that her daughter's life had been dismissed as worth about the same as a second-hand stereo. And still the woman doctor had shown no sign of remorse.

For the first time in her life my sister loathed someone.

I'm travelling with my sister to visit our parents, and I'm wondering whether she and I can possibly have any contribution to make to an anthology on sisters. We're a couple of chubby little women with wrinkled Celtic skin and broad bums and even though we may not have looked alike once, now anyone would know at a glance that we are sisters.

My sister is driving. She has only started driving again in the last few years and though we're moving faster than we used to on the way to the ping pong evenings, I'm reminded of those drives.

'I'll stop at Paraparaumu,' she says, 'because there's a service station on the left that's easy to get in and out of. I just hope we've enough petrol to get there.' I lean to look at the fuel gauge and it says half-full, which delights me. Paraparaumu is just a few kilometres away.

Further on we approach the rural turn-off to where the woman doctor lives. I know this because my sister has pointed it out on previous journeys, has told me that she sends a card each year on the anniversary of Catherine's accident. This is staggeringly out of character. I had asked, did the woman ever reply? My sister said no.

This time as we pass the turn-off my sister tells me that the woman has left. She has gone to live on the Australian Gold Coast. 'I wrote to her,' she says, keeping her eyes on the road. 'I said she'll like it there. We have quite a lot of relations living there and they like it. I wanted her to think she might bump into them.'

It makes me laugh aloud, but my sister still looks serious.

'Do you think that's . . . sort of crazy behaviour?'

I tell her yes, I do. A bit crazy.

And I feel inordinately proud of her.

KERI HULME

I Aim Carefully

Keri Hulme was born in 1947 in Christchurch, New Zealand, and is of Māori (Kai Tahu), Orkney Scots and Lancashire English ancestry. She has identified most strongly with her Māori origins and lives on the West Coast of New Zealand's South Island, where, among other things, she fishes for whitebait. Her first novel *The Bone People* won the Booker-McConnell Prize in1985. Her first collection of poems appeared in 1982, followed by *Lost Possessions* (1985), *Homeplaces* (with the late Robin Morrison, in 1990) and *Strands* (1992). She has also published a collection of short stories *Te Kaihau: the Windeater* (1986). She is currently completing work on a new novel *Bait.*

I aim carefully
between the dolphins that swim
in an airy gyre and
the flying pink pig

and throw the bottle at the hearth.
It's okay: it's made of plastic. It just bounces smack among the pile of junk I've got ready to burn. I turn my attention back to the keyboard —

'What will Diane be doing, this minute? She may be having tea with her fifteen-year-old daughter. She may be chatting on the phone to either of her grown sons who live away from the North Canterbury beach where her home is. She may be out, doing pre- or post-natal visits, or delivering a woman. She might just be feeding the cats, or thinking about the golden lab she's going to get soon.

'And Mary? Far away on the other side of the Tasman, in a country city in New South Wales, Mary might be at work, taking care of those whose minds have gone (or were never properly developed in the first place). She might be playing with her dog (a husky bitch with amazing pale eyes), or sleeping, or pondering the ups and downs of her life, or making a solitary tea. I don't know her duty roster but, like us all, she's an owl, so it is most likely she's awake and doing.

'My youngest sister Kate may also be having tea with her husband and their seven-year-old. Or she could be feeding homeopathic remedies to Jake. Jake tends to odd illnesses but

rather enjoys the remedies (and they work). I think Jake is a hypochondriac — if a standard-bred poodle the size of a large calf can be one. Kate lives at the same beach as Diane, so she might be round there, chatting over work. (They're both domiciliary midwives, in practice together.)

'The distances between us vary, both the miles and the psychic spaces, but we are knit together. We are sisters.'

One of the unlovely things about having a writer in the family is the knowledge that she may mine her relations for character traits and narrative happenings and you can't answer in kind (assuming the family has only the one writer in it, of course) until the day arrives for obituary comment.

Frequently, you miss out even then.

Aware of this — but comforting myself that I am a writer of fantasy and fiction — I have always studiously avoided *using* any of my family in stories. Consciously avoided, that is. Words and phrases do get borrowed

— *I've just realised it was Diane who said 'deep brown eyes I could drown in'* —

and shadows of their experiences crop up. When it's non-fiction, essay or interview, I have taken care to run comments by my relations. But editorialising can distort what I say or write; large chunks get left out, comments that do not belong in proximity get welded together. 'But I didn't say that!' I wail to family objections. There it is in black and white, they answer, a little grimly. Or, I've got it *on tape*.

This is a little different. This is me, a New Zealander of nearly fifty (born 1947), writing as I will about some of the people who are dearest in the world to me, my sisters. I have talked a bit about this to them, floated the glimmer of ideas past, but ultimately it is *me* writing about *us*.

A word of warning: I *am* a fictioneer, a fantasist. I do not have a very good memory for all the past, because I deliberately, selectively, recall what happened, and I deliberately, selectively, heighten what my reactions and sensations were, how the surrounding components of people and environment were, and I change the outcomes according to whim or desire. And there are personal spaces I will *not* trespass upon.

My sisters — Diane, the sister-next-to-me (in all kinds of ways); Mary, who has spent much of her time away from the rest of us, away from her siblings, away from New Zealand; and Kate, the pōtiki, youngest of us all, Kate the redhead with a core of intractable gentleness and determination — my sisters, each one of them, would tell very different stories.

I have two brothers, also.

Incidentally, there are signs on my back and front fences that read

UNKNOWN CATS AND DOGS
WILL BE SHOT ON SIGHT.

I'm sort of joking.

Indeed, for years I've been meaning to add another sign, to wit

HOWEVER, ANACONDAS, CETACEANS, BONOBOS AND LOXODONTS (SINGLE ONLY PLEASE) VERY WELCOME!

Just to show I really am a warm fuzzy pet-lover at *heart*, eh? It is quite important to know that our father died at an early age, when he was forty-two, in 1958.

I am the eldest, mātāmua, the first. Goodness knows what the families expected, but what they got was me.

The families were very different. My father John's people came from the north of England, round Lancashire, in 1912. They were working folk with adaptability and ambition. John was born in New Zealand, youngest of seven and the only male (now, *there* is a story of sisters!). He was indulged, charming and very, very egotistical. He was also bright, with entrepreneurial flair and considerable skills in carpentry and decoration, social manipulation and all-round organisational abilities. (The latter two saw him President of the New Brighton Businessmen's Association *and* the Workingmen's Club at the time of his death, and one of the youngest JPs created.)

He knew he was going to die early. (He had been diagnosed as having a 'weak' heart when he entered the air force. Which is why he wound up a supplies sergeant, home-bound, instead of being what his will and nature directed him to be, a fighter-pilot.)

That was one of the reasons he made my mother, Mary, both trustee *and* executrix of his will, and taught her to drive (this is the fifties, remember), and involved her great organisational and number skills in his business.

He knew he was going to die early. That is why he went full tilt at everything, building up the New Brighton Cash

Timber Supplies and the New Brighton Land and Real Estate Agency during the day, working until dark most nights, and then renovating the house we lived in for most of my childhood (he taught my mother what he knew of wallpapering and painting — and he had done his trades in that), and cultivating the gardens and the orchard, building a woodshed and a garage and a henhouse (which is where I learned about my father's fear and hatred of rats) and laying drives . . . Sometimes, in dreams, I take up where he left off, repainting the army hut, reroping the swings, realigning the main gravelled drive — it is a never-ending sequence, remaking childhood homes.

He knew he was going to die early. This is one of the reasons I have at least two half-siblings I will probably never meet.

Odds are, one of them is a sister.

My mother was eighteen when she met my father. He was twenty-nine, and already engaged, indeed had been engaged for several years. They married when she was nineteen, and I was born just after she turned twenty. We're both Pisceans. So was my Nana, her mother Mary.

Nana was the eldest of seven children born in New Zealand to an Orkney Island couple. They'd been small shopkeepers in Kirkwall, Mainland. They farmed when they arrived here.

Nana was known as a consummate horsewoman in days when a great number of people rode and dealt with horses. She was tiny, direct, very blonde (we have Norse and Faroese

ancestry too), very hardworking and indomitable. Educated only to primary school level, she went into domestic service as a kitchen maid when she was twelve, and wound up as housekeeper to a large station in Otago.

My grandfather Tom was a big, quiet, easy-going man, a stockman and a drover. He was a middle child of a family of fourteen. He courted my Nana for several years (while his younger brother Arthur courted her younger sister Florence), and married her when they were both in their late twenties. I know my grandfather was very gentle, and a great gardener. I know he had a desire, ever unfulfilled, to be a blacksmith. He put a notice on the front gate of their home in Oamaru which told the world what he thought of his family and his place:

TE WHARE O TE RĀWHITI

The house of sunshine.
My granddad was Kai Tahu.

Mary, my mother, was the second child of Mary and Tom's family of three. She, like a lot of second children, is both secure and a bit diffident, relaxed and compassionate, somehow intrinsically happier than her elder brother.

I know about this: I am the first, the eldest, and Diane is the sister next to me.

Mary is also very socially skilled — with *everybody*, from small frightened Aboriginal children to Prime Ministers of New Zealand; from schizophrenics to patronising know-all academics; from roughneck hoons to kuia who don't want to know te reo Pākehā (and Mary doesn't speak Māori), and with all her extraordinarily varied children and their mates and offspring. She is artistic, in calligraphy and sewing and knitting, in creating homes and in the cooking and presentation of food. (If you don't think these are arts, friend, you lack couth.) She is a great reader, and interested in most of what goes on.

My mother is a best friend. To me, to us all.

My father was a great reader too. And, like Mary, he was myopic.

You want to know the kids?

Look at the parentage, look at the bloodlines, look at whakapapa.

Of course, that fifty per cent of the genes my siblings and I derive from each of our parents may not be precisely the *same* fifty per cent. Given the rather large range of characteristics, physical and mental, that we display, it almost certainly isn't.

What are the estimates concerning personal make-up? Forty per cent genetic, and the rest environmental? Something like that for ordinary (non-multiple birth) siblings.

I *love* looking at whakapapa, hereditariness if you like. I love looking in front at what was, and seeing it surround me as what is, and may be.

It is one of the quirks of existence that I alone of all my siblings, for many years, pursued a profound interest in taha

Māori. The Kai Tahu side of my family has fascinated me since early childhood — walking beaches is enhanced considerably by the knowledge that the bones over the fence in the urupā walked the same beach centuries earlier. They would have seen the same kind of birds, eaten the same kind of kina and kūtai, called the reef Tikoraki and the island Maukiekie, and felt the same joy watching the sun come up over te moananui a Kiwa, a new day warming with light.

Those bones are part of me —
dissolving in the quiet black earth
cool calcined white where the wind found them
bloody and bright under the skin
that foots alongside Kiwa's sea

— walking beaches is something I have done since I could walk. Learning about the Māori side of my family started shortly after.

The quirkiness comes from the fact that I am the least Māori-looking of my siblings. (O yeah? What about that red-haired sister? Well, there's a prominent urukehu strain running through the whakapapa, redheads all over the place.) Although a cousin of mine, looking at my solid body with unnecessarily malign enthusiasm (I thought) said, 'You know, stripped down, you have an unequivocally Polynesian skeleton. I could wire you up alongside exhibit 33a and, aside from the freshness, no bugger could tell the difference.' That rocker jaw, he said rubbing his hands, those long thigh bones. I'm sure it was all meant reassuringly.

Curiously, as two of my sisters grow older, taha Māori grows in importance for them. Diane and Kate have attended several hui for Māori midwives, and have become interested in allied matters — kawa, tikanga Māori, as well as whakapapa — as a result.

There are a number of traits we all share. Short-sightedness, for instance (we all need corrective lenses for everyday life), is obviously genetically based. Other things are more mysterious in origin. I can see why we have

intelligence

physical competency (we are healthy, by and large — aside from the marked family tendency to drop dead from heart attacks and strokes — and naturally deft: we are well-built people, with fast reactions and good stamina)

and a drive to both accomplish, and do whatever we do, well.

We've inherited these qualities. It's probable that the

deep sense of justice (what is tika, right, fair play)

readiness to try new things or situations or people, underlain by

cynicism or unreadiness to believe until a matter is pragmatically proven

I often wonder at the weird aptness of my father's family motto

Fide sed cui vide

(aside from anything else, short-sightedness has appeared in that family for many generations!)

and the self-control, stillness/waitingness, ability to listen, we all have,

are both genetically and environmentally given. The interest in, and commitment to, family we share can be a bit overwhelming for people who are outside, as it were, but it is quite explicable: when my father finally died of heart disease, my mother was thirty-one. Her six children ranged from eleven to one in years. We all bonded tightly. We had to. It continues. It shows.

Our quick, pattery, rather light voices; our broad general knowledge; our dislike of eating certain kinds of offal (there was one memorably traumatic meal our mother cooked us, lamb brains in white sauce, which we have tried hard to forget) — I think I can see why we have these in common. It's the differences that increasingly fascinate me.

A lot of spiders hunt across my raw timber ceiling. Dozens of other squat motionless in their intricate webs. My house-crickets chirrup sweetly from the aloe vera and the avocado. Ichneumon wasps haunt the rafters and giraffe weevils are frequent visitors. On a good summer day, literally dozens of cicadas will sing in through one door or window, perch and stridulate awhile, then sing on out the opposite side . . .

Diane's house has a large number of wonderfully rampant potplants, and its share of spiders, but she doesn't tolerate the degree of webbiness and wildlife I have.

Mary would spray any trespassing insect or spider to death. Immediately. (Mind you, she does live in Australia.) She is not at all fond of disorder. (She would find my interest in moulds and fungi growing on last month's dishes for instance, horrifying.)

Kate's place is immaculate. There may be a spider somewhere inside, but it won't be anywhere obvious. (However, if her son has been on a frog-collecting binge, you can have surprising encounters in the bathroom. He also collects ghouls. And aliens. Seven, remember.)

I am obsessed by fishing.

Some of my siblings *like* fishing.

I am always inhabited by (Graham Greene's words) 'a small splinter of ice'. I am always watching and observant of self and surroundings, no matter how involved I may be, no matter how emotionally intense the occurrence. Part of me is apart from it all, even when I'm barely conscious or shickered entirely.

My sisters tend to be whole-hearted, whole-minded, wholly involved.

I am a loner by nature.

My sisters are very social, sociable, and socialised (although each of them also needs time and space to herself alone).

I am, by inclination, extremely lazy. I enjoy doing nothing.

I think my sisters are workaholics (so are my brothers). I admit they know how to relax, know how to party up large. And, they have responsibilities I don't have, so they have to work harder than I do. But where I'd be happy just to fish

creatively (for dreams or fins, ideas or views), all day every day when I wasn't sleeping, they need — a little more stimulation.

Maybe that is a key: I am extraordinarily self-sufficient while my sisters, happily for the human race (for they are, by and large, benign and generous folk), need other people for happiness.

On the other hand, who am I kidding? Take away my family (heaven forfend — I am not religious, nor particularly superstitious, just given to certain prophylactic phrases), take away my sisters, and there is very little *me* left . . .

And certainly no heart left for living.

When I was younger, much younger, I used to fantasise futures, not only for myself but for all of us. They were simple futures initially, based on my limited knowledge and experience.

> *Diane really likes Scotty dogs, so when she grows up she'll have half a dozen of them in beautiful kennels for her kids to play with. And their names will be**

They were futures dense with the assumptions children make — that people stay the same, that you really do know what your sisters want (in fact, that you really do *know* your sisters), and that only good things happen to good people, because they're good.

Not that I didn't play, early on, with picturesque tragedies (which always turned out well, with everybody becoming not only better but also better off than they were before). I was

*names for the dogs, not the kids

adept, too, at bare-faced channelling of aggression, particularly into what I thought of as 'other space' (I had been reading about alien worlds and alternative realities long before I was ten):

> *and Mary's room has a food dispenser that she can get anything she likes from — melting moments, cordial, anything — and there's a spare bunk for that horrible friend of hers, and whatever they think of will appear like a film for them. They'll be quite happy, and whenever they want to come back here, I'll release the door-seal. If I feel like it.*

They were fluid adaptable fancies, fed and enlarged both by everyday life and everything I learned.

> *It must be possible to invent a substance which is exceedingly thin and invisible and which will replace the layer of skin that Kate, as a redhead, lacks. A spray-on film, perhaps, or something you could add to the shower-water. Then she could stay out in the sun with no problems. Actually, if it could be made for everybody, then if you wanted to be browner or whiter or — blue!** — you could be, and the stuff made removable, so you could change whenever you wanted.*

**I've played over the years with this snippet — blueness in humans — uncovering examples ranging from Krishna to the Blue Men of the Minch. Thus, the race of Krsa in *On Shadowside* has a rather long prehistory in my imagination. (There's a Krsa in *Bait* too, but exceptionally well-disguised, unless you've really read that paragraph, in which case the game is given away.)

Fantasising futures became less fun with the years. Reality cramped my style. Increasing knowledge, self-knowledge as well as general knowledge about the depths and strangenesses and perversities of humanity, made me realise how superficial my future-making was, how sanitised and thin. I learned that we are vulnerable and frail in ways we don't suspect (until disaster befalls us). I learned that we dance along a razor's edge, largely unaware, and all my future-making became anxious, too, as though thinking about dooms prevented them from happening.

Maybe that much was true. Nothing I fantasised has ever come to be.

It is obvious that family relationships aren't static. Everything that lives, changes: everything flows, and not necessarily towards the good. Accidents of fortune can alter established hierarchies. Hope denied, or illness, can change personality. Newly unveiled strengths — or weakness — can shatter previous understandings.

The years act on us all like sandstone on pounemu, grinding down, eroding, shaping, polishing, destroying. He mahi hōaka, te mahi tākata — and all that remains in the end is dust.

That's an interesting whakatauākī, by the by: it's normally used to indicate that those who work for people (as in 'serving the tribe') are ultimately ground down by it. But it also means, I am told, that *any* relationship, any dealings between people, work as hōaka (sandstone) on pounemu. Raw greenstone has its own kind of beauty: shaped greenstone must needs encounter the grindstone.

It's just as well we cannot truly know futures. I used to play with tarot cards and palm-reading, and, like most people who delve conscientiously into such matters, have had my share of inexplicably correct foretellings. Although none of my siblings is religious, some do have an interest in alternative medicine, and the occult fringe (I am deliberately running the two fields together because in practice they frequently overlap), and a wary belief in — no, not as strong as that, a guarded openness as to the possibility of — a spiritual side to humanity.

We have come to be mature adults through very different experiences. While my experiences, prediction 'hits' in tarot and palmistry notwithstanding, lead me to accept the finiteness and physicality of the human personality, my sisters' experiences have led them in a slightly different direction.

Then again, my sisters, all three of them, have seen people born and people die, and I've never been privy to either event . . .

So, here we are, me on one coast of the South Island, Diane and Kate on the other; we three here in New Zealand, and Mary in Australia. The distances exist, but are ameliorated by that most human ability, talking —

We all like talking. We gossip. We chat. (This goes for the entire family: a clan gathering of Hulmes, spouses, children, hangers-on, is essentially a talk-fest). We go in for long loonnng telephone sessions.

Not necessarily the four of us together. There have always been pairings-off in my family: Diane and I (we shared the same room for many years, and frequently the same bed until

we were ten or so), Mary and Kate (they shared the same room when Mary was home, she being brought up partly by our Nana and our Uncle Bill), and the boys. The pairings changed, as circumstances changed, although such changes didn't eradicate the initial pairing: Andrew and Kate grew very close after Mary left for Australia, John and Mary grew very close because they were both in Australia. Mary and Kate again, when Kate lived for some time in Australia (is not proximity essential to knowing someone well?), and Diane and Kate, as their shared dedication to midwifery became dominant. Diane has always been, for me, the closest sister. She trusted and supported me right from the time she could talk. I'm not sure the trust was well placed, to begin with.

> *Diane, two-ish, has picked up a really effective swear-word. She proudly chants it, and is told off.*
>
> *Me (with regrettable smugness): Isn't she a bad wee bugger for swearing?*

And then there was the time of the fires . . .

We shifted into our home at Leaver Terrace when I was five. Then, it was surrounded by bush, and we kids used it as *our* playground (as if Leaver Terrace wasn't large enough, over two acres of it). We were resentful when sections were surveyed (in fact, we made ourselves obnoxious by first pulling up the survey pegs and, later, ruining the foundation pegs) and the bush started to be cleared. There was a spectacular explosion one morning when contractors blew up a huge tree (I can still smell the cordite and the bleeding gum). The ruins of our playground were scraped together in many large stacks and fired. The pyres burned all night.

A day or so later, Diane asked me whether it was okay to walk on yet. I blandly assured her it was. I'd already set several pieces of cardboard alight by tucking them under the ash layer . . .

Trustingly, barefoot, she set out (but not very far). Shoes? We had a thing about shoes. We delighted in bare feet. I can still remember the first time I melted frost with my bare feet. Yeah, it was cold but how extraordinary — I am so warm my feet can melt ice!

And my mother still recollects with embarrassment being approached by the head teacher of our primary school, not long after John died.

He said diffidently, tactfully, 'We appreciate how difficult it must be, Mrs Hulme.' Fred Price was a truly kindly man. 'We have funds that . . . can be used?'

'What for?' asks my bewildered mother.

'Well, you know, necessary things that might be a bit difficult to provide now. Six young children after all, and we know how fast they grow.'

'*What?*'

'Shoes,' said Fred Price succinctly.

We were not popular for a while.

We'd been stuffing our sandals into the milkbox each morning (it was a large milkbox because we got four quarts of milk a day), and traipsing happily off to school barefoot. Awww, the poor little orphans. With native cunning and an inborn sense of self-preservation, we'd put our sandals back on before turning up inside our home.

Our mother was not amused.

I won't say I led that particular escapade, but because I was the eldest and very much boss-child, I was responsible for a lot of strife.

There's Mary sobbing her heart out, and my mother concerned as to why: the kid looks unharmed, and the rest of us are playing quietly together in a corner of the sunroom.

'Whatever's the matter?'

'They won't let me come with them!'

'Who?'

'Them!'

Diane and I. We went off to Never-never Land, our vehicle a ping-pong ball, tiny airy chariot most suitable for travellers who could condense themselves to flickers of light — see on the wall there? There? *There* (swiftly palming the bit of metal that produced the shimmer) — and had marvellous adventures with Tinkerbell (who was enhanced way beyond J.M. Barrie's wisp — she could fish, for starters). We told Mary all about it, in great excluding detail. Well, I told Mary all about it while Diane loyally corroborated. I was the storyteller (and I had the inside knowledge about Never-never Land, having learned to read while very young).

A two-year-old hates to be excluded. A two-year-old will believe absolutely anything. And I distinctly recall, watching the ruckus with satisfaction, that I'd proved points to myself about both matters.

It wasn't all petty betrayals and mind-bending games. Far from it. I enjoyed straight storytelling to my siblings, and reading to them. I liked drawing pictures for them, and co-operatively creating new games. Leaver Terrace was a superb place for apple fights in the orchard (woe betide you if you *picked* your ammunition — anyway, green fruit didn't squish so satisfyingly on the targets), for tree-huts in the huge macrocarpa hedge, for hide-and-go-seek round the army hut and the asparagus bed (which was actually a rampant asparagus forest). Moeraki provided different joys — we invented the tide game, made increasingly sophisticated things from kelp (balls, bags, slippers), and built strange habitations and constructions around the cliffs and caves. At Oamaru, we dressed up in ancient frail clothes that had belonged to our great-aunts, or marauded (discreetly) in Uncle Bill's shed; raced carts down Lune Street and fished off the harbour wharves.

Indoors, wherever we were, cards and board games ruled — Ludo, Monopoly, snakes & ladders, Chinese checkers. And chess.

Our Uncle Raynee had taught me to play, while teaching himself the moves (from the *Book of Knowledge*, as I recall, an eight-volume compendium I feasted on when small). When I won the second game, he stopped teaching me, but I'd caught the bug, and duly passed it along. It's an odd game, chess. The more you play it, the more enjoyable it becomes. It stays in the mind at the stage you leave it, ready to be picked up and advanced, decades later if you so choose. It appeals to certain personalities much more than others and I could (but won't) divide my siblings up into natural chess-lovers — and others.

Scrabble is another watershed sort of game: two of my sisters aren't particularly fond of it (although we all play it quite well, having better than average vocabularies). Kate and

I (and my mother and Andrew) go in for Scrabble tournaments, hours long. We're both seven-letter specialists (in fact, the Kate manoeuvre is very well-known and abhorred in the family — the devastating ploy of going out with your seven-letter word at the last moment, trapping everybody else with lots of redundant tiles); we both take the game seriously (that interesting little fizz of anger when someone places a word in the space you've patiently cultivated), and we both like to win. There was a game at Okarito that has become legendary: she won the draw, and laid out a seven to begin with. Hey, good opening move, but it didn't cause me as much consternation as she might have liked, because I laid out my seven in response. And leant cheerfully back. How's about that eh? And turned into a stunned mullet as she put down *another* seven-letter word. (She ultimately won, too.)

Another activity (and I use the word with deliberation) we all love, is reading. Give any of us a good book, and you can kiss conversation goodbye. In fact, you can kiss almost any kind of response goodbye.

One of my sisters is deeply engaged with a novel. She's been reading for nearly three hours. Her kid has been whingeing for the past hour. 'Shss, shss,' she says, absentmindedly, at intervals. He starts bawling (he's hungry). The stridency eventually penetrates and she snaps, 'Oh go find yourself a book and be *quiet*!' Sniffing resignedly, the kid goes. He knows what kind of family he's come into . . .

Why didn't I do anything, play good aunt instead of amused observer? Well, for one thing he wasn't starving. For another, I was reading too. And, for the third, there is one noticeable and prominent difference between my sisters and myself: I am not at all maternal, parental even. I just don't have that instinct to nurture.

Don't get me wrong: I care, and care deeply, that family children grow up happily and well. On rare occasions, I've looked after them. But, whereas Diane and Mary and Kate eagerly, by choice, one way or another have a lot to do with kids, I, eagerly, by choice, don't. Hell, I don't even think they're human until they can talk properly.

There is another obvious and substantial difference. All my sisters are, or have been, married, and I've never been in the least intimate with anyone (in *that* sense of intimacy), and this is a matter both of inclination and deliberation.

Oh yes, over the years I've thought about whys and wherefores. At one time, I simply concluded the human sexual continuum includes natural neuters and I'm one (while being physiologically normally female). Relatively recent research into the pre-natal influence of testosterone provides another possibility, however: female foetuses exposed to higher than normal levels of testosterone in the uterus (whether because the mother is taking the hormone or because of foetal abnormality) show, as adults, certain traits and abilities. Greater spatial and mathematical ability than most women, much less relationship commitment, social isolation, lack of interest in offspring, and a greater propensity to dominate.

I rearrange shapes (rooms, puzzle forms, small engines) in my head, and I accurately gauge distance (in imperial

measurements still!). I used to enjoy mathematics very much (until I struck a school teacher who ruined the pleasure). And the rest of it . . . yeah.

There is an oddity though. Like most of my family, I have to gesture physically, refer to my hands, before I can tell which way is right, which way is left.

Sisters. Different —

I had just returned from a long barefoot walk on Moeraki beaches. Sitting down outside the crib Eldersley, I brushed sand and gravel off my feet, and noted with pleasure how hard my soles were. I said as much to Mary, Hey, I've got good calluses.

She shuddered. I don't want any calluses.

That's idiotic. You won't be able to be comfortable walking barefoot.

There's more important things than walking barefoot. Your feet have to look nice.

Mine do.

I thought she was impractical. She thought I was weird.

but understanding, as the years accrue, that the differences can be matters of insight and appreciation rather than matters to separate and antagonise.

Sisters. Each supporting one another in our individual styles, in the ways we have learned, or think, or at least hope, will help each other most —

It had been a miserable year for me. I was writing fulltime, but had nothing ready to publish, I was unemployed and all grant applications had failed. I was living with

Diane and her husband, and their two kids, and while I relished the hospitality, I felt awkward about it. I couldn't contribute much. I hated being in the least dependent.

Diane knew it. For the festive dinner that year's end, she made two things that were to my strange tastes entirely. One was champagne cocktails, lovely lethal drinks that delicately, definitely annihilated — woes, worries, feelings of inadequacy (eventually, all feeling!). And the other was atholl brose . . .

Atholl Brose is a Scots concoction, honey, oat water and whisky. I love those flavours separately or mixed, and my sister knew it.

Diane's version was a Christmas pudding, melted honey and a lot of whisky blended with hard-whipped cream, sprinkled with toasted oat flakes and chilled.

Nobody else ate beyond a taste, the whisky being too strong for them. I relished it, for its luscious quality and, most of all, for the underlying savour of subtle tautoko and sisterly kindness —

So. Here I sit, writing about my sisters, writing about me as a sister.

Storytelling, as usual. And I know about stories: they can meander and drift, and they can flourish in eye-poppingly surprising ways; they can stain with sadness, or make your heart balloon with joy. Sometimes, their course is inevitable. Other times, they mutate and burgeon beyond the teller's will or control.

And all stories end.

Genes go on. Books may live long. Memories continue in

unforeseen ways, and the shadows of actions, some people believe, influence the future to an unguessable course. All I know is that Diane, and Mary, and Kate, and me (and all our family) are, for now, a continuing story and I dearly love the characters. The plot's a good one, and while I would have changed some nuances in some chapters — well, I'm writer enough to know that no story is new in this world, or alone in its genesis. And no writer ever controls everything.

Hē aha te mea nui?

Ka kī au, he tākata, he tākata, he tākata.

The worst thing I can imagine for any being is absolute aloneness. People, for people, are the greatest thing. And my sisters, my family, are unequivocally the greatest thing in my life —

I wish it were so, for everybody.

The silver dolphins jig overhead.

And over there, flies a pig —

Margaret Mahy

Stories, Songs and Sisters

Margaret Mahy was born in New Zealand in 1936 , the oldest of a family of five, and spent her school years in Whakatane. She worked in the School Library Service before becoming a full-time writer specialising in children's books. She has published extensively in the trade book area as well as in various educational series, including among her titles *The Changeover* (1985) and *Memory* (1987) for older children. For younger children *A Lion in the Meadow* (1969) and *The Witch in the Cherry Tree* (1976) remain favourites. Her many awards include the Carnegie Medal, the Esther Glen Medal, the New Zealand Literary Fund Award for Achievement, the AIM Junior Book Award, an Honor-ary Doctorate of Letters and the Order of New Zealand.

A Story

I went into the waiting room. For a moment I had the whole room to myself, but then the door opened again, and first one and then another woman came in after me. 'Select a number and take your places,' said a voice echoing through the p.a. system, so I took a number from the machine. Number 1! I was first. The shorter of the two women behind me, the one with the knitted hat and the jacket lined with sheepskin, took Number 2, while the third woman, with the clean, crisp shirt and the tidy hair, took Number 3.

I had brought a book with me, but somehow it seemed too unfriendly to begin reading immediately.

'It's a little like being in a lift,' I said to them. 'I mean — here we are, thrown together at random, and it seems as if we should *say* something meaningful, tell a joke, perhaps, or sing a chorus before we shoot off in different directions again.' The taller of the two women smiled a little, and began to sing.

She had a dark and a roving e-ey-eye
And her hair hung down in ring-a-lets.

I knew the song so well, and I didn't hesitate to join in. But I was surprised when the second woman, the smaller one, sang too. It was, in a way, what I've often dreamed of — people surrendering, all in a moment, to the impulsive release of song and dance.

She was a nice girl — a proper girl —
But one of the roving kind.

Then we all laughed, having exchanged intricate information coded into an apparent simplicity.

'I hope we won't have to wait too long,' I said. 'I've a pile of work waiting for me beside the word processor.'

'I've got to collect my pig food,' said the smaller woman.

'This is my private time of day,' said the third woman. She had a deeper, slower voice than any other in the room. 'I want to get out into the garden. And I'm making a patchwork quilt. I hope they don't keep us waiting too long.'

The door opened and a fourth woman entered. Just for a moment I thought I knew her. She was younger than the rest of us, with pretty hair — looked as if she were about forty, twenty years younger than me. She paused, glancing from one of us to another as if she, too, felt we had all met before under some softer light.

'Take a number please, and wait your turn,' said the crackling voice of the p.a. system.

She took a number from the machine and looked at it.

'Number 5,' she said, looking at the three people ahead of her and then back to her number. 'Who's missing?'

We considered the mystery of Number 4. And, as I looked around, in case Number 4 was hiding in some corner, I saw that the waiting room was equipped with a small bar.

'Well, we can't be waiting to see a doctor,' I said. 'Anyone want a drink?'

They all refused, smiling a little as I poured myself a gin and tonic. I could see tolerance, along with an edge of criticism, in their smiles. With the drink I immediately felt easiness flood through me, along with the illusion of being eloquent, witty and free. I looked around the room, down at myself, then over at the other three women.

'I'm a writer,' I volunteered. 'I mean I make my living at

writing. I began writing when I was seven, and first saw my name in print when I was about eight. When I was nineteen or twenty (when I was too old to be a child myself and before I had any children of my own) I began to write children's books. By now, I am nearly sixty years old. I have two daughters and two granddaughters. Back in 1961 I was what was called an unmarried mother, but the simple passage of time has turned me into a solo parent.

'These days I begin writing early in the morning, surrounded by cats while, in the background, the *BBC World News* plays on an old television set which once belonged to my aunt. The images are not always clear. Colour comes and goes according to rules I don't understand, but its randomness seems more convincing than the definition of better functioning sets. I sit at my word processor, and behind me I hear voices giving an account of the world. People perform atrocities on one another out of deeply felt convictions, and the voices report on this and on cars, fashion, and current films.

'I hear remarkable things. A space-shuttle flight has been cancelled because of attack by woodpeckers. I turn, and see men marching around the space-shuttle tooting horns and holding up a false owl on a stick to frighten woodpeckers away. Or I hear that Idi Amin was so impressed with whisky that he gave Scotsmen the right to enter Uganda without passports. Can that be true? Spinning in my chair, I catch a picture of Idi Amin marching along, resplendent in a kilt. I am writing about incongruity as a source of humour, and it seems that the *BBC World News* is colluding with me. Later in

the day I will be mother and grandmother, gardener and dog owner, but at 4 a.m., with the cat asleep on the fax machine and someone behind me interviewing a man who has married his dog, I am a writer wondering how invention can ever have anything like the edge and variety of real life.'

I fall silent and see the eyes of Numbers 3 and 5 turn towards Number 2. She hasn't had the advantage of a drink, but my own gossiping voice has made it easy for her to talk too.

'I am three years younger than you,' she said. 'I have a degree in accountancy, which seems to put me into an entirely different category from yours. People tend to speak of accountants as if they were mechanical systems constructed in the form of human beings. Yet a good accountant knows as many secrets as a priest. Money can be as highly personal as sex. Those figures, trustingly submitted to me, stand for someone's work . . . time . . . their secret *life*. They stand for the choices a person has made, and the energy they put into fulfilling the choice. I don't know that I actually chose to be an accountant out of any real interest. My father saw accountancy as a desirable career for a capable girl, and I fell in with his wishes. After all, I was only fifteen when I finished my seventh form year, and, almost at once, I left home, and began boarding in Auckland, working for a prestigious firm of tax consultants and studying for an accountancy degree.

'But these days I am only a part-time accountant. I own land, along with horses, cows, hens and pigs — a miniature farm. I get up early in the morning, and carry buckets of sloppy pig food down a slope, across a stream, and up the slope on the other side to my pig unit. The little pigs look out from their house with a kind of shy sweetness, then charge in on the food, while I hose out their pen, cleaning it for the day ahead. Sometimes I let them out of their pen, and they are so excited that they dance with pleasure. People don't always realise that little pigs can leap and play like lambs when the world outside opens up to them.

'It is part of the nature of that outside world that there are mornings when I hate what I have to do, but when you are dealing with animals reduced to dependency, you have no choice. No matter how cold it is, no matter that the slopes I must cross may be lashed by bitter rain while the stream runs high, I must feed my pigs and hens, not to mention the cats. I have about twenty cats at present, all neutered, cats that have been abandoned on the roadside, or passed over to me, living their own lives at ankle height, a sub-culture filled with friendships and feuds. Some choose to live in the house, others prefer the cowshed. Some hunt rats and rabbits and require almost no keep; others are older and more dependent.

'In some ways I wish I had found out earlier that I wanted to live this sort of life. I was married once, but now, as I live on my own, I grow fonder and fonder of solitude, though I have good friends, and a daughter who runs a chicken farm. We live close to one another so we are in constant touch. I ride with friends, compete in dressage and jumping events, and love my horses. But it is a very different life from the life I thought I would have, when I was at school, one of a group projected from Standard 4 straight into Form 2. In my final

year at school I was swimming and tennis champion as well as being top of the class. I had a competitive spirit and competed well. But now I have an existence made magical in ways I could not have imagined. I am the rider my older sister always longed to be, the chieftainess of a tribe of cats.'

'Well, I have a daughter and two sons, three grandchildren and two more on the way,' said the third woman. 'I live next door to the very house I grew up in, and sometimes I walk into that house, look around and think with amazement that I have undergone some change of dimension. There were once seven of us — five children and two parents — all living in these small rooms, though they didn't feel unduly crowded back then. My father built the house at the time he and my mother were planning to get married. "This house will still be here in a hundred years," he told her, choosing well-seasoned wood, and building with love, though without what we would, these days, call "style". I remember my mother cleaning these box-like rooms day after day, and by now I have cleaned them many times myself. I was the one who took over where my mother left off.

'Sometimes, at night, we children would turn out the lights, scatter and hide in the darkness. "Worraworra!" one of us, the seeker, would call. "Worraworra!" four voices would reply from various rooms of the house, and the search would begin.

'There were things about me my parents were not prepared for. They were not prepared for someone who began to take an interest in boys at about thirteen or fourteen, someone who wanted to bleach her hair and promenade around town on a Friday night. They did not expect a child who would argue with them in quite the way I argued, who did not automatically accept their axioms of behaviour. Riding confidently on the music of Elvis Presley and the first rock-and-roll bands, I surged towards adult life, misunderstanding the anguish parents feel as their children tear themselves out of the flesh of the family and go in contrary directions. And even if I had understood, it wouldn't have made any difference. I had chosen a different life from the one they would have chosen for me.

'I married at about eighteen — a boy I had loved for a long time. He was Maori, shy and silent in the presence of my parents, who were bewildered by his silence, for they did not feel so very formidable within themselves, though they had all the prejudice of their background and time. Yet, in due course, two things worked to modify this prejudice. I had children, and they could not resist the children. And then I was the one member of their family who stayed geographically close. The others dispersed, leading lives that, in the beginning at least, seemed to be lives my parents respected. But I was only a few miles away, and, as things became increasingly difficult, I was the one who was there to help. And besides, as even more years passed, I was suddenly able to feel the sort of curiosity they had expected me to feel back when I was thirteen. My oldest son and I did fifth form subjects together. "She has become her true self," my mother then said of me, but I had always been my true self, even if she had refused to count my early choices as truth.

'It hasn't been easy, but I am still married to the same man. After all sorts of collisions within the dance of marriage, we

are still whirling around, arm in arm, finding new closeness. After all, he and I know things about each other that no one else knows. Each of us is the repository of the other's essence. I don't mean that as romantically as it sounds. It is something both ordinary and remarkable, something that has to be worked for and *stayed* for, something which cannot be won except through persistence. I loved being a mother, and I love being a grandmother to such an extent that it is hard for me to accept that any life without children is a true life, so in an odd way I echo my own mother's declarations.

'I work every weekday as secretary to the principal of a large secondary school, listening to educational rhetoric and gossip with a certain derision. After school and in the weekend, I do light carpentry, make a little extra money upholstering chairs, or sewing curtains. I can work with stained glass or make bowls of papier mâché, which I paint in bright colours. I make dolls for family babies, patchwork quilts for brides, listen to beautiful music and garden. If I paint a room, I prepare it meticulously. I once had professional painters in, but they did not sand the old surface down as well as I would have done it. They didn't have the same feeling of *rightness* about what they were doing that I have, when I paint or garden or sew, so they can't have had the satisfactions either.

'In the end, I looked after my mother, making up to her for any grief she had ever felt on my behalf. And in the end, she and my husband understood one another in an unexpected way, because she had grown up during times when men were there to be respected, and he was the man of the house, so she respected him. When she died I was sitting beside her, to stroke her forehead and tidy her hair. Later my oldest sister and I mixed the ashes of our parents and buried them in the garden of the house that had been built to last a hundred years.'

She fell silent and we looked at each other with pleasure and puzzlement too.

'The time's gone quickly,' I said, and glanced, I couldn't help it, at the youngest one among us. She smiled as if she understood my glance was really a nudge, that I wanted her to speak too.

'I'm nearly fifty,' she said, which surprised me because I had thought she looked younger — not simply younger in the smoothness of skin or thickness of hair, but because of a certain openness of expression. 'I have two daughters — one at university, one in the fifth form. I live in a house on a hill with the father of my daughters. I am on call for two part-time jobs at a hospital for disadvantaged people, neither job totally reliable I suppose, but I know I am valued. The calls seem to come regularly and I never turn down the chance to work. After all, my father's highest praise for another man was to say that he was a good worker, and this emphasis on work became part of me and all my sisters. One of my jobs involves straight domestic work, and the other is caring for patients. I am an official *carer*, and some of them are so severely disadvantaged that they have to be cared for as if they were babies. I think it is important work, though, like a lot of important work (particularly women's work), the inner thread of excellence, of nobility too, tends to go unrecognised

even by other women. 'It's unqualified work,' an academic woman once exclaimed of work like mine only minutes after she had been complaining of marginalisation by a male hierarchy in her university department. All the same my work makes the world go round just as much as hers does.

'I had a lot of good commercial skills when I left school, but, while I took time off to have my two daughters, paper sizes changed and computers came in. I was a full-time mother for many years, partly because I thought, and still feel, that it was best for my daughters to have a home-based mother, and partly because I enjoyed our family life together so much. Perhaps I had directed myself towards this family life when I was a child, playing house in the hedge around home, making tiny rooms between the trunks of the hedge trees, then climbing into upper branches to make a second storey. I was fond of my dolls (though in the context of the game I could fuss over a log of wood with total conviction), and in adult life I liked making things for the girls (dresses and aprons appliquéd with birds and flowers) and for my home.

'At times I have been really poor and desperately worried about money but there are great victories within the context of poverty. The good bargain gained in some thrift shop — a desired second-hand book located among the Mills and Boons, or a remnant of linen that will make into a good dress — these are triumphs, true pleasures. I'd never say that money does not matter — I know there have been times when everyone in my family has blessed the benefaction of family money: the energy of my father's long working life passed on to us — but I chose for my daughters and myself that we should make our own way with a kind of simplicity, and I think that we are close and resilient and strong partly because of what flows through me from my own childhood and partly because of what I have been able to invent as I went along.

'For a long time I would bike through the city in all weathers from home to work and then back again, and people sometimes used to exclaim at the distance, because so many people think a car is a necessity. Now we do have a car, and I love the new ease and the extension of possibility, and yet there were things I enjoyed about the bicycle — not just the exercise, but a certain feeling of achievement. Sometimes I would sing as I rode. I love singing and dancing, and cycling, if you are in the mood for it, is a sort of dance. I wish I could sing so that other people really enjoyed listening to me, but I sing anyway, like my eldest sister, who is even worse at singing than I am.

'My partner is a halfway practical man — that is, he is practical enough to get ideas and to carry them through halfway, so we live among projects begun and never finished. Sometimes it is wearing to live like that, but after a while it gives life a dissolving edge that I can quite enjoy.

'I was the youngest of a family of five. Ten years separated me from my oldest sister. We were a family of readers, children engulfed by story. By the time I was eight my oldest sister was working and then left town to go to university. I *almost* remember the family circus she organised (I hung by my knees from a trapeze that hooked onto a trapeze the older

children used). By now, that circus seems quite a useful image for our family lives. Like clowns we shouted and aimed blows at each other, but we also reached out, like trapeze artists, to catch the hands of someone hanging mid-air before they tumbled out of reach.'

As we had talked the light had faded outside, and the world beyond the window looked dark. It was hard to tell, taking the various accounts into consideration, just what we were there for. Presumably we had come together because we had something in common, but the various lives we had outlined — the lives of writer, farmer, latter-day scholar, and homemaker seemed to have only vague connections. Yet, looking from face to face, I saw something I knew — something *remembered.*

She had a dark and a roving e-ey-eye . . . one of us sang, and suddenly we all knew what we were seeing. We recognised one another. We were sisters.

All together again, we cried to one another, embracing. *All together again.*

Whatever had brought us to that room, whatever we were waiting for, was forgotten. The others were happy to celebrate now, so we filled glasses with champagne from the bar and talked with ease, almost timelessly, it seemed, about the present and the past, about our shared childhood, our children and grandchildren, our parents and our lives in the small, square house that had been built to last a hundred years. Every now and then I suppose we became aware that we had very different opinions about the world (after all, we were different people who had led different lives), but when moments of possible contention cropped up we would laugh and shrug, sing the old songs, and repeat the words of old nonsense games. After all, I had known these women for longer than anyone alive had ever known them. There was no one left to remember their beginnings as I did, no one left to remember me as they remembered me. So I became myself with them, my present and my historical self, in a profound and unspoken way quite impossible with other people more passionately loved. I felt *true* in this company.

Suddenly a door opened, not the door we'd come in by. We turned and saw the long folds of a curtain with a shadowy passage beyond it.

'Would the client holding card Number 1 come through now?' said the voice of the p.a. system.

I looked at the card in my hand.

'Just when we were having a good time,' said Cecily.

'Let them wait,' said Patricia.

'After all, they've made us wait,' said Helen.

'Oldest first,' I said. 'But we'll catch up with one another sometime soon.' I moved over to the curtain. Then I paused. I looked back at them. 'Worraworra!' I said. 'Try to find me!'

Slipping behind the curtain, I walked into the darkness beyond.

Songs and Games

The preceding story is part of a longer story, one which began many years earlier, and it is a story of sisters. Brothers have primacy in the Bible. They crop up in Chapter 4 of Genesis in the St James translation and, though Cain and Abel are hardly positive examples of sibling engagement, they exemplify a recent speculation in the *New Scientist* regarding genetic rivalry between brothers and sisters. Indeed over and over again these days, mothers of second babies are made aware of the probability, even the inevitability, of sibling rivalry, and the *New Scientist* backs them up. Jealousy has come to seem so mandatory, that failure to admit to its existence suggests delusion. Nevertheless I do not remember feeling anything but excitement and rejoicing as my sisters made their consecutive appearances. The sophistications of jealousy may have surged in later, but I say, confessing to a simplicity which may not have been quite what it seems, that I rejoiced to be a sister. Indeed, some time after the last of us was born, speaking on behalf of myself and my two older sisters, I begged my mother to have yet another baby, an invitation she turned down, using my father's age (he was over fifty at the time) as an excuse. And I must say that, though I loved the idea of another little one in the house, I don't think I had any real intention of being useful in a domestic capacity.

I come from a family dominated by women. Not only am I the oldest of four sisters, but I am the mother of two, and these days I watch my sibling granddaughters with fascination, noting how the younger of the two is entranced by the cleverness and skills of the one above her. They inhabit a knee-high world, into which an adult can peer only by falling on all fours, rather like Alice, grown large, peering with one eye through the little door 'into the prettiest garden you ever saw'. For a while I had a version of a similar garden all to myself. For three and a half years I was an only child, invested with the charm of novelty by parents who were easily able to convince me I was beautiful and clever. My sisters, however, have always had to share, and I imagine there was a time when they studied me with the same sort of sharp interest and awareness of possibility I detect in my younger granddaughter as she watches her bigger, stronger, older sister scrambling effortlessly onto the trampoline.

I seem to remember — I do remember — the excitement and drama of the various arrivals of each of my sisters, of my mother's return after an absence of a week or ten days, carrying a baby firmly wrapped in a white shawl, and the mysterious enjoyment of seeing first one sister and then another feeding at our mother's breast. It was not too different from the pleasure I felt when I first saw a cat lapping milk.

Perhaps I am remembering the same baby over and over again, but no — it is not quite as simple as that. I was so excited when the third of us came home, so noisy and rumbustical, that my father sent me outside when the moment came for the baby to be fed, and I lay, weeping under a lemon tree, excluded from a family mystery.

First me! Then Helen, with whom I share so many of my early memories, followed by Patricia and then the one of us excluded from this particular account, my brother Frank. And finally — shortly after Frank — Cecily, the one with naturally curly hair! There are three and a half years between me and Helen, and another three and a half between Helen and Patricia. After that, an apparently well-ordered system broke down. There are a mere two years between Patricia and Frank, eighteen months between Frank and Cecily.

My mother was certainly self-conscious about having another baby quite so soon after the last. Both my grandmothers, mothers of six children in one case and seven in the other, were scornful of people who had large families. It looked too uncontrolled, too *Catholic* my mother said later, lowering her voice a little, and she did not immediately tell her own sisters (she was the youngest of a family of six girls) about the new sister in our house. Letters were regular, but visits were few, and it was not difficult to hide Cecily's presence for a while. But then a cousin of my mother's paid an unexpected visit, and, after he and his wife had left us, there was a flurry of phoning. There was embarrassment, but no great shame in my mother's voice. She laughed at her double weakness — that of having had a fifth baby so soon after the fourth, and of having tried to keep it a secret. And there we were, four sisters and a brother, a span of ten years between first and last. All so similar and all so different.

My mother says that as a scrambling toddler, I drove her mad. I ran away not just once but over and over again. She shut the gate, but I learned to open it. She tied it tightly, but I learned to climb over it, and off I ran, out into the world with complete confidence of arriving at some desirable *other* place. During the latter part of her second pregnancy my mother often wondered (she told me), 'What on earth am I going through all this again for?' A year and a half after asking herself this despairing question she looked out of a window and saw her second daughter racing off towards the gate. 'Here we go again,' she thought, racing away herself, only to find that Helen had shut the gate and was coming back again. My mother quoted this in a wondering way — the moment when she realised just how different sisters can be. I was made eccentric by unrepentant ego, reinforced by largely uncritical love, Helen turned out to be clever and capable, while Patricia grew to be rebellious. As for Cecily, she seemed to me to contain in her own imaginative choices some echo of my own obsessions reinvented and made her own. We described, not a circle, but a continuous helical twist.

The essence of our shared childhood has become a mystery, coded into songs, stories and games. I can remember, when I was about six years old, marching round and round the table with Helen close behind me, both of us shouting a repetitive nonsense chant:

As he marching EEZ-A-MOR! EEZ-A-MOR! EEZ-A-MOR!
As he marching EEZ-A-MOR!
On the capital day of December.

The words, my own invention, grew out of the act of marching, and Helen, then aged about three, seemed delighted to chant with me and march behind me.

A few years later, after our lights were out, Helen and I would organise 'radio programmes', calling and singing to each other through the open door between our bedrooms, in low thrilling voices, inventing radio serials, songs and musical links. 'Dum-duh-DUM dum! And now the news!'

Regularly we joked and wrestled, working ourselves into that state of hysterical entertainment known as 'getting the giggles', and giggling at the meal table ('silly giggling' my mother would exclaim irritably, worn down by the percussion of shrill voices in a small room) was forbidden. ('Please, *please*, let's have a little peace and quiet. Stop that silly giggling!') Yet somehow, being forbidden, giggling became imperative. Helen and I, then later Helen, Patricia and I, would sit with heads bowed, in a state of inner agony, not daring to glance at each other. With despair I would feel a rebellious squeak force its way through my compressed lips, and then answering snorts and snuffles from Helen and Patricia. Mostly in the end, unwillingly and a little despairingly, our parents would laugh themselves, and when that happened we could join in openly, and set ourselves free from the fearsome pressure within.

Helen and I, as we grew older, regularly made pikelets — and then evolved an elaborate game that we played at the table as we ate them. We would pretend to be two posh women sitting in a tearoom and sharing a plate of cream cakes (the aristocrats among contemporary cakes). We would talk about the delicious flavour and social pre-eminence of our own cakes and the contemptible nature of mere pikelets, nibbling our pikelets, until only a crumb remained between thumb and forefinger. Then, after a glance of agreement, we would stare intently at our respective crumbs and, taking our time from one another, gasp and cry out in a horrified duet, 'PIKELET!' This game seems to me to involve not only social commentary, but to suggest the essence of a family ritual, developed and polished through repetition.

We all climbed trees. I think I was the most enthusiastic climber going from tree to tree, checking birds' nests, unable to believe that the presence of anyone so well intentioned was likely to put any stress on the birds, but my sisters also climbed, made caves and tunnels in the hedges around our home, and played a surrealistic version of the game called 'house'. Cecily had dolls she was fond of, but, along with friends from next door, mothered logs of wood as happily as she did the dolls. Trees were the constant companions of our childhood.

Our father hung a trapeze from a pine branch and we put on a circus attended by indulgent neighbours. I was Daniel de Haven, the originator of the event, organizer and ringmaster, snapping a whip made of clothesline rope with a piece of frayed string plaited into the end so that it would crack appropriately. Helen was the star of trapeze, Patricia was clown as well as trapeze artist, Cecily, aged about two, hung by her knees from a little trapeze, also made by my father, which hooked onto the bar of the big one. Helen, Patricia and Cecily grew clever at turning cartwheels, at skipping and skating. I was never as well co-ordinated and, compared with any of my sisters, I am still clumsy. But,

being older, I was often in charge of the games, and the words that gave them form.

In some ways we lived dangerously. I always liked to swim out beyond my depth and lured my sisters to swim after me. To be in danger, but confident, proved our mastery over the water. My mother, watching us set off to the river, probably never really imagined that I would swim Patricia, possibly before she could safely swim the distance herself, to the opposite bank and back again, supporting her whenever she grew tired. None of us drowned, but perhaps that was good luck. Somehow, once in the water we felt adventurous, and more than adventurous — we felt immortal.

Finding ourselves alone in the house, we would sometimes turn out the lights and become inhabitants of darkness. 'Worraworra!' we would shout, like Tigger in the story from *The House at Pooh Corner*, and one of us would crawl through the darkness trying to find the others by touch or the sound of breathing and stifled giggling. Given the chance and right circumstances, we would still be happy to turn out the lights and hunt one another through a darkened house.

It was years before we owned a car, and when we visited my Awakeri cousins, or went to see bridges that my father was building or drove over the hill to Ohope Beach, Helen and I travelled on the back of my father's truck without any constraints except our parent's strict instructions that we were never to stand up. As we sat on the back of the truck we sang. Cecily and I, these days, are at one in finding song a profound pleasure in our lives, though we both sing badly. Indeed if I was to be offered a wish — a wish that I was to spend only on myself — I think that the ability to sing pleasantly would be my first choice, though thicker hair would come a close second. Cecily, who already has thicker hair, would almost certainly choose to sing.

On the back of the truck, though, first two of us, then three of us, and finally all five of us sang without inhibition, finally working out a cycle of songs. *She had a dark and a roving eye, There's a pawn shop on the corner of Pittsburgh Pennsylvania, The bog down in our valley oh, Three juvenile delinquents* — all songs that precede the dramatic advent of rock and roll. The choice of songs was dictated, I think, by me, since, though I was a bad singer, I remembered words so well, and liked lively, comic songs in the music hall tradition, or songs that told stories. As Helen and I did the dishes we sang another cycle of songs deriding teachers and neighbours who had annoyed us. The words were our own, but the tunes were those of familiar songs — *The Ash Grove* or *The Minstrel Boy*. Other songs praised our own cleverness and the family we came from.

Any evening any day,
If you go down Haig Street way
You'll find us all (oy!)
Doing the Mahy trot!

Or when we were older travelling to tennis matches (for we all played tennis), we would sing to the tune of *The Happy Wanderer*, which was then a popular song on the radio —

I love to go a-tennising upon the tennis courts
And standing on the service line, I look my best in shorts.

Fifteen love . . .
Thirty love . . .
Forty love . . . And it's game, ah ha ha ha ha!
Thirty love . . .
Forty love . . .
With an ace I make it game.

Singing and playing games — it all sounds idyllic, the sort of thing that makes politicians talk sentimentally about the days when families really *were* families, and children made their own fun. But, of course, that is a dangerous over-simplification and one often made by people anxious to turn the platonic ideal of family to their own advantage. After all, a certain sort of happiness in childhood, while it can make children strong, is a strange preparation for the ferocities of adult life. Sometimes, now, our past happiness seems like a fairy tale, almost an aberration, real in itself, but giving no intimation of our probable future lives. We were all to encounter savage despair in love, the area in which we were constructed to be most faithful.

In due course, Helen, who came directly after me, did become a rival in a way. We entered on a time when we argued incessantly, though I find it impossible to remember what we actually argued about. I picked on Helen, watching her with a constant critical eye, ready to pounce. I can also remember some jealousy when she began to write stories of her own, and I recall deriding her story to my mother, who pointed out that she, my mother, could say some of the same derisive things about the stories I had written, but chose not to. Perhaps I had already marked literature as my own area, had concluded that I was the person born to be in charge of the story. Perhaps I expected Helen to listen to my stories, with no intention of listening to hers in return.

I went through primary school in low classes but Helen always did well — often enormously well — at school. I don't remember resenting this in any way. On the whole I was proud of her success, though puzzled by my own failure, which persisted until I reached secondary school. I was a highly proficient reader, I wrote good compositions (as writing exercises were called in my days) and I gave lively morning talks. But in those days, neatness and accuracy were probably more highly prized than they are today. Helen was not only apt at self-expression, able to remember well, capable at mathematics and less likely to be distracted, but she was also neat and well controlled in the mechanics of writing and spelling. In infancy she shut the gate tidily after her, and at school she pressed lightly on the page with her sharpened pencil, just as we were supposed to do. None of the rest of us did as well at school, and Helen's success, which so delighted my parents, altered expectations for those who came after her. When I went through school there was no one ahead of me against whom I needed to be measured, but this was not the case for either Patricia or Cecily.

I tried to dominate Helen, but she refused to be dominated, though, in turn, she tried to dominate Patricia, at which stage I took Patricia's part in the family squabbles. Patricia seldom intruded on the territory I thought of as

mine. Helen argued with Patricia, but took the side of our little brother Frank, who, several years later, apparently bossed Cecily around and tried out all kinds of tricks, holds and torments on her. But by that time I was away, a student at university, virtually a visitor in my childhood home.

In a way, I now think, I fell in love with my own childhood of songs, games and adventures, and I think I tried to stay with it for as long as possible. I felt none of the excitement and pride my own mother apparently felt when, totally unenlightened by her own mother, she finally understood the reproductive facts of life. What I felt, when the information was forced on me, was profound dismay. But, retaining childhood for myself involved the restriction of my sisters to childhood as well, and I became repressive and judgemental of their choices as they reached for adulthood.

Adolescence caused us to become strongly differentiated. My brother, a child as talkative as any of the rest of us, retreated to the sort of silence approved of in males of my family, and admired in New Zealand generally. My mother certainly approved of his new, mature, masculine silence. We sisters, though increasingly aware that our judgement never quite had the authority of our brother's where our mother was concerned, were at least allowed to talk — to gossip, argue, criticise and express feelings. My brother was expected to conceal his.

I tried organising the family imagination wherever possible, even after I left home, and, with the willing complicity of my parents, I organised the idea of family and loyalty to tradition along fairly inflexible lines. I did not want our Christmas — the tree in the house, the presents under the tree, the shared opening of stockings in the morning — to change, for Christmas significantly encapsulated the general happiness of my childhood. I remember it as an ecstatic time, when I overflowed with feelings of love and with a flawless pleasure. I was furious when, in due course, I found Patricia was planning to spend Christmas Eve in town with her friends. I needed her presence in the house to be happy myself, so I lectured her on loyalty. I openly attacked her decision in a far more dictatorial way than either of my parents, though they were certainly taken aback by her sexual persona, which became individual and assertive when she was about thirteen or fourteen. I had refused to wear lipstick or put on make-up myself until I was about nineteen or twenty, and I needed the agreement of those around me, a resolution similar to mine, in order to stop the flow of time. Deviation seemed like treachery. But even in adolescence, even in early adulthood, 'Worraworra!' we would cry, turning out the lights and feeling for each other behind doors, under beds and through wardrobes.

'I have always been worried,' writes A. S. Byatt in the acknowledgments at the end of her book *The Djinn in the Nightingale's Eye* 'at being the eldest of three sisters.' But I am the eldest of four, the eldest of the fairy tale triumverate plus one more, doomed by the determinism of fairy tales to make wrong choices. And my own worry, a curious worry since there is nothing that can be done about it now, is that I loomed over the three that came after me rather like a djinn, at times directing their lives by something rather

sharper than example — by expecting them to act within the confinements of characters in my private story. But they have all turned out to be heroines in their own stories. And we are all still participants in a family game. 'Worraworra!' they cry to me from their various shadowy concealments, and I crawl through darkness, trying to find them, listening for their breathing and smothered laughter.

MARILYN DUCKWORTH

Cherries on a Plate

Marilyn Duckworth OBE was born in Auckland, New Zealand, in 1935 but spent a wartime childhood in England. She has published 12 novels since her first appeared in the UK in 1959. These include *A Barbarous Tongue* (Award for Achievement), *Disorderly Conduct* (New Zealand Book Awards 1985), *Unlawful Entry, Seeing Red* and in 1995 *Leather Wings*. A short story collection *Explosions on the Sun* was published in 1989. She has held the Katherine Mansfield Fellowship in Menton, a Fulbright Visiting Writer's Fellowship and university fellowships in Wellington and Auckland. In 1994, she held a summer writing fellowship in Hawthornden Castle in Scotland and in 1995 the Sargeson Fellowship in Auckland.

Who's that knocking at the garden gate?
Little Fleur and Marilyn with cherries on a plate.

I rang my sister last week and she was enthusing about a hedgehog she had found living in her garden. She welcomes temporary residents — of the bird and insect variety — in her East Finchley home. One year she introduced me to a spider, Tiger, resident in her pantry and last year a family of robins nesting under the roof. When I reported this typical wildlife conversation to our mother, Irene, she pointed out to me that hedgehogs eat snails. I'm not sure where Fleur's loyalties lie as far as snails go these days. In the sixties she wrote a poem, much anthologised and lauded, which concludes — 'And we are kind to snails.' Indeed, and to slugs as well. I remember a busy summer morning spent rescuing distressed slugs from the edges of our tent and washing them clean of DDT in our rain barrel. We were nine and ten and camping on our lawn in Sidcup, Kent. It was Fleur who taught me never to kill a spider but to catch and deposit it outside. I used to have nightmares in which she picked up a hairy spider saying, 'Look — it doesn't bite!' Then her face would twist with shock and topple sideways to die. Fleur's death was one of my worst fears.

When interviewers ask the inevitable question, 'Are you and your sister literary rivals?', I feel almost sorry for their ignorance. How could they ask such a question if they knew anything about our childhood, our loyalty to each other? My answer is easy: 'She's a poet and I'm a novelist — she lives in London, I live in Wellington.' Supposing we had been two London novelists, could we have been mutually hostile like Margaret Drabble and Antonia Byatt? I can't believe it.

There were the usual childhood rivalries, some of them extending into early adulthood. As a child I was convinced that she was the more loved by our parents or at least the more admired. I didn't think this was very unfair, just a fact. She was eighteen when she left home to be a married woman. I was sixteen and still at school. Around the same time my closest friend left school for a job in a library. I felt abandoned. Travelling around England during the war, changing homes and schools suddenly and regularly, I was used to losing friends out of my life, but losing Fleur was a shock I wasn't prepared for. I wrote about this feeling in a Virago short story, *A Game of Pretend.*

> *For the time being I was shut out of Hester's [Fleur's] bedroom while she and her fiancé filled the room with smoke and other fuggy smells. I was shy about making noises in the next door bathroom and learned how to spit toothpaste foam soundlessly. On the day of the wedding the house was cluttered with visiting relations and I was transferred to a campbed in a small space. I didn't mind. It wasn't until all the relations were departed and the campbed folded up in the cupboard that I noticed what had happened. Hester had gone. Not just for a holiday. Gone. And I had forgotten to prepare myself for it. Her clothes had gone from the wardrobe. I could spit as noisily as I liked. I don't remember crying. It was worse than that. There is a phrase —*

'My belly thinks my throat's been cut.' Yes — that describes the feeling well enough I think. Emptied out, closed off.

That year I would arrive home from school and my mother would dart out of the kitchen, her face expectant and alight. Then 'Oh — it's you.' Fleur had become a visitor. I didn't doubt that my mother loved me but I could tell there was a difference. The only thing to do was to marry and become a visitor myself, which I duly did. Too hastily, as it turned out.

I visit Fleur in East Finchley as often as I can. We respect each other's rituals and feel amused by people who consider us odd. We occupy separate kitchens in her house, mine a cold-water kitchen converted from her son Andrew's photographic darkroom. Fleur eats her vegetarian meal at 7 o'clock, listening to *The Archers*. I eat my cottage pie watching *Coronation Street* or *Eastenders* at 7.30. In the old days we would have sat side by side at a table with books propped against a teapot. Although she lives in London, she has become increasingly rural while I have become increasingly urban. We stride around the English countryside in comfortable boots, looking for late daffodils and bluebells. (I'm obsessed with catching the bluebell season but seem to just miss it every year.) Fleur walks faster than me — I push myself to keep up with her, as I spent my childhood doing. I was always two steps behind, which corresponds roughly to the number of years between us. I stroll around the city on my own; Fleur hates the West End and the underground. Nearly every time I visit England we make at least one pilgrimage to places out of our childhood or to explore the villages of distant ancestors. This is one of Fleur's

obsessions. I enjoy orienting myself in the history of my forebears but I'm glad Fleur, the ex-librarian, does all the research for me. I respect her quest for knowledge and the past and her talent for accuracy.

Our childhood was much concerned with 'truth'. The legacy of that shared obsession is still with me today, reflected in my life as writer, as friend, as wife. It seems to me that, rather than lies, there are too many approximations of the truth. I'm always searching for the exact truth of what was said, felt, done.

It all goes back to Fleur. 'Have you got the light out?' my mother would call up the stairs at bedtime. Fleur would leap to the switch, respond, then flick it back on and return to her book. The truth, you see. This taught me not to be satisfied with quick, easy answers. But it wasn't only the letter of the law that mattered to us so far as truth was concerned. We were deeply moral as children — I like to think we still are. We would trust each other not to spy on secret writings or look for hidden birthday presents. 'I trust you,' Fleur would say, fixing me with her eye, and that was it. I couldn't look and never broke that trust. I don't believe she ever broke my trust when I laid it on her with the same heaviness.

There were other ways of being cruel. 'I know Marilyn can be irritating,' my mother would say to Fleur, 'but you mustn't bite her.' I don't know even now in what way I was irritating but I'm sure I was. I sustained a few bites.

We arrived in England from New Zealand in 1939 just after the declaration of war (we had been on the water when the news came). I was three and a half and Fleur was five. She was enrolled at St Gertrude's Convent with some kind nuns, leaving me at home to play childhood games alone. I had a little brown cardboard lunchcase like Fleur's. I pretended I was at school — it was lunchtime — I attacked the case with a knife and fork. It was so boring being a lone sister at three and a half. When Fleur came home she dared me to do wees behind the armchair and laughed when I obeyed and got into trouble.

Our parents were both employed at the Ambulance Depot. A horrid woman we called Mrs Rubbish came to mind us and clean the house. Margaret Shaw, the sixteen-year-old daughter of a friend at the depot, would visit and join us in a game we had invented called 'lick tongues'. She was the only person who would play it with us. The startling sensation of tongue on tongue was a delight to us, but our mother was discouraging. She was discouraging, too, when I pointed out to Fleur the delicious feeling that could be obtained from riding the arm of the sofa. When I asked why not, she just went on dusting the piano keys quite noisily.

We lived close to the twin ideas of war and survival, only dimly apprehending them. On the mantelpiece there was a glass cylinder containing a surgical needle and catgut to break in case of an emergency. We had been given Bakelite identity discs to wear around our necks, inscribed with our names and addresses, in case of air raids. One morning Fleur and I were sitting at the dining room table labouring to write our dolls' names on the back of their necks while Irene, our mother, was raking out embers from the grate. Suddenly we saw the back of her blue smock was on fire. Fleur had been

taught what to do in a fire. She yelled, 'Lie down, Mummy. Lie down!' She wrapped the mat around my startled mother and whacked at the flames.

I never doubted Fleur's wisdom. When I came across knowledge she didn't have I was always amazed. I knew our family was special and I knew Fleur was better and wiser than anyone else's sister. It didn't surprise me when she became successful overnight as a poet in London. We had both planned on fame as writers, from about age nine or ten. One model was a children's novel, *The Far Distant Oxus*, which was written in tandem by two teenage girls and sent to a publisher by Arthur Ransome, before the war. Our mother pointed out the wartime paper shortage which made early publication unlikely, but she allowed us our aspirations.

It is very difficult for me to talk about my childhood without talking about Fleur's, and equally difficult for me to write about Fleur's childhood without writing about myself. Who had which ideas? Where did she end and I begin?

Sidcup was only a short distance outside London and the raids were getting closer. It was arranged that we be sent to our father's relations, Eva and George Carter in Melton Mowbray, which was in Leicestershire. I was four and a half when we drove up the private road to their farm. There were two children in the family, much older than us — Jean was ten and Betty was fourteen. They both wore round wire framed glasses just like Aunty Eva. The house was built in an L shape and Grandma Carter lived in the back part of the L. In the courtyard there was a water pump guarded by a black barking dog. Rover. Fleur said she wasn't scared of Rover. In the big smelly outside lavatory, with a vast wooden seat from wall to wall, there was a child's commode. We were made to sit on it for useless minutes at a time. In the dining room there were multi-coloured rag rugs made by Aunty Eva, the same colours as the tiddly winks we played with on the baize-covered table. There were gas mantles in the downstairs rooms but we had to take candles when we climbed the stairs for bed.

We played in the spinney, a little wood behind the cowshed and chicken-runs. We had pink smocked dresses for best and for 'chapel'. At the Sunday School party Fleur and I sang *Away in a Manger* and recited a poem we had made up with help from our mother, Irene.

Who's that knocking at the garden gate?
Little Fleur and Marilyn with cherries on a plate.
Let them in, 'cos it isn't very late.

Our lives were full of rhymes and rituals, both our own and from books. I can still recite lunatic rhymes made up by Fleur, while she surprises me by quoting gibberish verses of mine. There was a swing behind the Carters' house. I would swing by myself for hours at a time, talking 'poetry' of my own making, a senseless scribbling of words together. I learned later that Fleur did something the same. Irene could make our skin tingle when she recited the poem 'Nymph, nymph, what are your beads? Green glass goblin — why do you stare at them?' I feel a familiar tingle writing the words now.

We attended the local school at Scalford. I wasn't yet five. I was scared of the place — of the stuffy smell of chalk and

the hot breath rising from the Horlicks we were given at lunchtime. We had to bring our own mugs from home. Fleur told me how to ask the teacher if I wanted to 'do wees'.

After school Fleur read *Jerry of St Winifreds* in the sitting room — it was a Sunday School prize. I was given a book about Brownies and tried to read it. Fleur told me to 'Shut up, you can't read!', and I believed her.

I kept asking when we were going home. Irene would come sometimes and bath me in a basin on the bathroom floor, which I loved because I had her to myself. What upset me most was not being able to say goodbye to her without people looking on, watching me cry.

At last we learned we weren't ever going 'home'. We were going to live upstairs in a house in Surrey with some people called Rogers. Our mother would be there and sometimes our father too. They had come to take us there. At dinner I became self-conscious about eating in front of people, which was a recent neurosis. My plums and custard were put on the piano until I finished my stew and new potatoes, which I couldn't. Fleur was disgusted — she never left food on her plate. We left in the dark the next morning before the hens had laid eggs for our breakfast.

At the Rogers' place in Honeycrock Lane we had to sleep top and tail. There were a number of air raids and I would wake to find myself being carried downstairs with a pillow to shelter under the Rogers' dining-room table. Fleur was always wide awake and knowledgeable about what was going on. Our parents' bedroom was also our living room and cosy with cooking smells. Some weekends my father came home and made peanut butter from roast peanuts. It tasted burnt and gritty but we loved it. One day he brought home a packet of small, round orange jubes. He told us these were 'lollies' — the first sweets I remember. We were entranced. We were only allowed one, after dinner so as not to 'spoil our teeth'.

That winter Fleur and I ate muddy ice off puddles on the common. Fleur was usually the one to take risks with what she put in her mouth, but this time I agreed with her that the ice looked delicious. Perhaps it reminded us of the water ices we had had in New Zealand. We spent the next day in bed, sick. The outside loo was a long way away. It was distempered, with newspaper squares hanging on a nail. I had to stand on the wooden seat to reach the chain. Irene showed us how to scrumple up the paper to soften it so that it didn't scratch your bum.

Outside was a garden with a deep hole where an air-raid shelter had been spaded out but not finished. We found a burst bag of chimney sweeper's soot in the unfinished shelter and rubbed it on our faces. We were 'Secret Exploring Indians'. Fleur's idea. (Later she resuscitated this club to impress friends at a new home.)

Betty Rogers, who was thirteen, was impressed by our naughtiness. We played with her and her cousin Meg. Meg's sister had been killed in a car accident and at the time of the tragedy both girls had been given dolls to console them. When we were leaving the Rogers' place, they came and ceremoniously handed us the dolls, giving away the bad memory. It seemed to me the dolls were sad. Pixie Ann was

a big soft doll with a china head and a sweet smile on a sculpted mouth. Miranda was a dainty cloth doll with a cardboard head and 'real' ash blonde hair. Fleur had already conned me into swapping our baby dolls because she coveted the one with eyelashes. She didn't want another doll, so I was allowed to adopt both these orphans. Fleur was good at sewing and made clever garments for her two smart dolls. She also tried her hand at making rag dolls, so I found myself with another two sad, floppy little dolls to love and worry about as well. In this way I went through my childhood, collecting dolls and responsibility. I was careful to love them all equally and to teach them about life. For, as I wrote once in a poem, 'How could I send them ignorant in the world that terrified me?' Fleur told me Pixie Ann had once been a real little girl. Her father had pretended he was going to take her photograph and when she smiled for him he had shot her and had her stuffed. The implications of this story upset me deeply. I tried not to believe it.

Outwood was south of the old village of Bletchingley, buried in the country. The house we rented was called Top Lodge and was the lodge of a big estate. There was a long private gravel drive leading away to the 'big house'. Our house was beyond a maze of rhododendron bushes inside the main gateway. The sitting room had other people's furniture in it, which was beautiful, but we had to be very careful not to jump on it. There was a long padded piano stool with curved handles. The outside toilet nurtured big spiders in the notched walls. The forest of pinetrees to one side we called the Teddy Bears' Wood, which made it seem less dark. Across the drive there were armies of tall horse daisies and fields where we found enormous squashy evil toadstools, buzzing with bluebottles. It was summer.

Soon after we arrived we stumbled upon a soldiers' camp directly next door. Our parents were disturbed by this discovery, but we made friends with the Major and Johnny, a handsome sergeant who became a friend of our maid Doris. Doris moved in with us to look after Fleur and me while Irene went on her insurance run on a high bicycle in Bletchingley and Horley.

The school bus drove us to Outwood School. We had hot milk at playtime and had to bring our own cocoa and sugar in little tins. Fleur had a horror of the skin on top of the milk. She had a number of these phobias — wet paper, hairs in her food. I respected these but they weren't my horrors; I had my own. There were smells that frightened me, and a sensation I called 'the big and little feeling'. And snakes, of course.

At playtime the boys chased us into the girls' lavatories. If we were caught they would tickle us, which was unbelievably awful. After school one day Fleur and I and a girl called Irene, our mother's name, hid behind the piano and showed each other our bottoms. We were exact copies of each other.

One day at the school bus stop I complained about my cough. Fleur said hers was much worse. Next day the doctor said I had whooping cough. I stayed home for weeks and slept for a time in my mother's double bed. When I was getting better, I learned to wander about Outwood on my own, looking askance at bloodsuckers on the white

shepherds' purse, and smelling the 'stinking nannies', a sort of daisy. I visited the soldiers and had billy tea with them and went for rides in the Major's open car to the end of the drive. I relished having experiences Fleur was missing out on. She had her revenge. She came home one day with bicycle grease on her leg from someone's bike and she told me she had left school and was working in a bicycle factory because of the war. At first I didn't believe her, but she went into such detail I began to wonder. She must have been seven at the time. I was nearly six.

At bedtime we prayed for the war to be over. We had a number of bedtime prayers, which grew as we acquired new friends to worry about. Aunty Eva had promised us they would visit when the war was over so we used to pretend they had come — it was a way of ending the war at least in our heads. We'd run inside shouting, 'Betty and Jean are here! The war must be over!', and we'd make the V for victory sign with our fingers, like Churchill. I liked Churchill because my father told me he couldn't learn his tables at school. One day we got tired of waiting for Betty and Jean. We chalked a notice on the road which said: ALL CARS STOP HERE. We hid in the hedge and waited for the cars to pull up. The Major came and told us off.

During the summer of 1979 we made a last pilgrimage to Outwood. As we came within view of where the house should be, we saw a deep shining space ahead of us, like a river. We puzzled and then as we came closer saw there was a motorway carving through what was left of our memories. We walked sadly on, looking for a pub or a teashop where we could get a drink, and came to 'the oldest working windmill in England'. There was a man on the gate welcoming tourists and we talked to him for a bit, explaining how we had once lived at Outwood and were now looking for a teashop. He called out to his brother:

'Hey, Jack! These young ladies used to live here thirty-seven years ago and they'd like a cup of tea!'

The war went on. We bought our own house, still in Surrey but in a built-up part, near the Salfords shops. All the houses in Woodside Way were similar but different. Hilltop was a semi-detached, three-up, three-down, with french doors opening onto the rockery and a tiny fishpond. There was a duckpond, too, at the bottom of the garden where hazelnuts grew. We acquired four ducks. Tui was mine, Weka was Fleur's. They were Khaki Campbells. We had two white ducks, Dilly and Dally, but they never became pets like Matilda, my mother's duck, who choked and died, or Ninny, our evacuee Joan's duck. Joan, evacuated from London, was older than Fleur and became another sister for the years she lived with us. My mother helped Joan sew me, out of an old brown felt hat, a duck I named after Tui. I added Tui happily to my collection of dependants; with so many of these it was sometimes difficult getting into bed at night. Fleur had only one bedtime companion — Bobbie, the twin of my dog Prince. She had hugged all the fur off him.

One night Irene discovered Fleur disobediently reading in bed and threatened to give me the tussore silk pyjamas she had been sewing for her. I was wickedly pleased. In fact,

Fleur got her pyjamas and a pair was made for me as well. At that time we had pink pinafore frocks starched so that they could stand up on the floor on their own. I had a red swirly patterned dress with an elastic waist. I would stare down at myself and think I was so skinny I might break in half. One Christmas a woman in the Ambulance Depot sent me a bright orange knitted frock with green buttons from top to hem. I wore it to school and showed off. Fleur told me I looked ridiculous. I'm not sure even now if she believed that. I'm reminded of another occasion when I was quite grown up, preening in some new garment, and Fleur's sudden stabbing comment — 'You've got the Robinson ankles.'

The first winter at Woodside Way the duckpond froze over. Fleur suggested I walk on it to see how strong it was. It wasn't strong at all. I sank to the bottom while Fleur choked with laughter and I think, remorse. I got ice in my knickers and had to have a hot bath.

One weekend Fleur and I cut staffs in the woods and went for a hike. We crossed the railway line, which was forbidden because of the dangerous electric rail, and walked towards Redhill, past the 'lunatic asylum', listening for sounds of madness. Approaching Earlswood, we stopped to explore a half dried-up stream. I slid and fell across a snake. It had a yellow mark on it so we decided it was an adder. This was the second snake I'd fallen on. Fleur used to tease me for my fear of snakes but she had to admit they seemed to follow me around. My clothes were wet with mud so she made me take them off and go home in my mackintosh with her ribbon tied round so it wouldn't fall open.

From Woodside Way we had to walk daily over the common to St John's School in Redhill. Fleur and I would never cry in school. On my first day in school I had felt desolate. Fleur was in the upper school, not the infants. I couldn't believe I'd been abandoned in a classroom among strangers, but I wouldn't cry.

At lunchtime Fleur and I played in the churchyard next to the school. One day we saw a grey squirrel up a tree and, since the bell had gone, she suggested we catch it and take it as our excuse for lateness. We spent hours making a trail of acorns leading into the church porch, to tempt it. We waited expectantly, whispering. We were very late and there was no squirrel. Fleur told me that other kids said 'the clock was wrong' but we were not to lie.

Fleur and I were both signed up for ballet lessons with a Miss Sharpe, who had been the first teacher of the Covent Garden ballerina, Beryl Grey. We wore little black tunics split at the sides, short-sleeved wrap-around bodices and black ballet shoes. We changed in a downstairs cloakroom in an exciting bustle of parents and other children. Fleur hated it. The first day we had to wear our smocked pink party dresses, which were too short. Early on, Miss Sharpe singled me out for having a nicely pointed toe. It was all the encouragement I needed: I pointed my feet madly. One day at dancing class Fleur and I were shocked and entranced to see a little girl wet her knickers noisily in the middle of a jeté. Fleur gave up ballet quite early but I continued and went for my Grade One exam. I did a hornpipe and a mime and a small ballet sequence. Every morning close on exam

time I practised while Fleur and Joan slept. I loved the music Irene played to accompany me. Fleur made up her own kind of dancing called Slidderiana, which you did in your socks on the lino floor. To compete with Slidderiana, I made up a language of my own called Grimtig, which was spoken in my invented land of Grimland. I sang carols in Grimtig.

Fleur and I went on to invent a shared land we called Dreamland, since the stories we told each other about it were part of our bedtime ritual. Gradually the stories became part of our daytime life as well. Misty Mooner and Katy Kildare and Mrs Frederick Gillis inhabited our conversation as if they were real. I don't remember being taken to Redhill library but I remember the books that somehow arrived in our home. One book concerned a witch called Fleur who sat upside down on the ceiling and a fairy called Marilyn. We thought this a wonderful coincidence and I was smugly pleased that I was the fairy and not the witch.

We received the occasional food parcel from New Zealand — once a tin of butter and shortbread, once a fruit cake with cherries. An old lady friend who was staying with us divided up the last of the cake and asked, 'Who wants the crumbs?' Fleur and Joan and I all cried, 'Me! Me!' She gave Fleur the crumbs but no cake. I was shocked. Cakes, even of the eggless, butterless sort, were a rare treat. Whenever we ate with other people I made it a habit to count the number of whatever was offered and match it up against the number of mouths. Fleur didn't seem to notice and would often take two of something which meant I had to say no thank you when the plate came to me. I couldn't bear to think of the last person being disappointed by an empty plate.

One summer holiday Fleur and I were sent to stay on Jacksons' farm, while our mother was employed working for 'the war effort'. Peter Jackson was older than Fleur. We didn't like him but we allowed him to teach us how to catch tiddlers. There was a drowned orchard with the tops of the trees visible and water spiders walking on the surface. The evil millpond was deeper than anyone had ever measured and we crossed the bridge alongside it, reverent with fear.

A year later I returned to the Jacksons' farm during a measles epidemic at my school. By this time I had been transferred from St John's to St Hilda's in Horley (our doctor's suggestion, to help my nightmares). I carried my luggage in Irene's round hatbox. She put me on the bus in Redhill and the driver put me off at the gate to the farm. It was my first trip alone. I was seven. I had a torch in my case for when I had nightmares — my father's bicycle lamp. I walked up the long lane on my own. On one side there were ponds completely covered with pale green scum that looked solid but I knew would collapse underfoot. I passed some gypsies camped in an old car by the side of the lane — fruit pickers. Peter was at school. The next day I wandered over the farm, exploring the fields of corn on the side Fleur and I hadn't visited. I sat on gates, leant against trees and made up poems and songs — 'I think that I will play no more, in Appledore, in Appledore.' I missed Fleur. I felt romantic and sad. I would go on messages to the village for Mrs Jackson and be given a chunky threepenny bit. My legs got very tired, but it was something to do.

On Saturday Peter Jackson told me to hide with him in an old shed so we could watch Mr Jackson mating the cow with the bull. We peered through a crack in the wall. I was astonished at the way Mr Jackson bullied the bull into clambering into an uncomfortable position on the cow and wondered why he didn't gore Mr Jackson when he got himself back down. I knew what they were doing and couldn't see why Peter was getting so excited about it. He suggested we go up in the loft above the bull's stall and try it for ourselves. I said maybe later. Every day he asked me and every day I said 'tomorrow'.

When I came home I told Fleur we had gone up in the bull loft and undressed, to impress her. She was impressed and promised not to tell. But she kept dropping hints about it in front of Irene and using it for blackmail purposes.

Fleur and Joan used to tell me ghost stories with the lights out and chant eerie verses at me when Irene was next door visiting a neighbour. They knew I was frightened of dogs but once they came with a little black puppy and dropped it on my bed. I squealed and the puppy jumped down, getting mixed up with the interminable scarf I was knitting. At this time I slept on a campbed in Irene's room because of my nightmares.

For some time Fleur had had a crush on Michael Glenny, a boy who caught the school bus. I invented a boy called Robin Manders whom I said lived next door to my school and used to meet me secretly. I fantasised about him for Fleur's benefit and she believed me. Years later in Ireland, when we were sharing a small bedroom in a Donegal guesthouse, I confessed the lie. She was furious.

The air raids were getting serious. There were doodlebugs and rockets. We had an Anderson table shelter with an iron top and a wirewove mattress base in our dining room. This was where we all slept, including, for a while, a little hunchback woman who had been bombed out down the road from us. Fleur and I would go to bed before the grown-ups and tell our Dreamland stories. One evening when the Morris kids were sharing an air raid with us — their mother was out — Fleur and I contemplated our small juicy thighs and wondered what human flesh might taste like. Kathleen Morris was shocked. Fleur is a vegetarian today.

I was eight and Fleur nearly ten when we were put on a train and sent again to stay with Aunty Eva and Uncle George on the Melton Mowbray farm. We went again to Scalford School. Fleur reclaimed the place confidently and was reprimanded for reading the headmaster's mail over his shoulder while she stood at his desk waiting for his attention. I counted this as my sixth school because, although we'd been there before, the people were all changed. I calculated my life in terms of people rather than places. Fleur was constant but other people kept running away from me or changing. Aunty Eva was grumpier than we had remembered her. I mooched around the redcurrant bushes, lay down and let bunches of them drop into my mouth. Grandma Carter in the side house told us a story about a little girl who ate poisonous berries

and died. I missed my dolls. I invented a secret home down a rabbit warren. There was a whole neighbourhood down there, I insisted, and when no one believed me I was surprised at their lack of imagination.

At last Irene came to fetch us, but again we weren't going home. She was working in an agricultural camp in Corsham and had found us separate billets in the little village of Hawthorn, not too far away.

There was no running water in any of the village houses. We had to go to the village tap to fill pails of water. I used to sit by the tap and watch the drips collecting when I was supposed to be fetching water for Mrs Whittington. At night there were two enamel pails set under the window of the one bedroom where we all slept. One pail was for piddling in, the other contained drinking water with a cup for dipping. I used neither — I was afraid of getting them mixed up in the dark. I envied Fleur. Her house was further away from the tap but her outside lavatory was closer to her back door. Not only was my sister living under another roof but she had a new name. Mrs Johnson had a small son who couldn't say Fleur's name so she had been rechristened Jean.

It felt very strange to be in a different family from Fleur. There was a feud between the two women. I was loyal to my 'family', but I missed Fleur. I'd been there for some weeks before I was taken away from Mrs Whittington's house and went thankfully to join Fleur in her tiny one-room-up and one-room-down cottage. The sofa was carried up the short flight of stairs to be my bed. Fleur had a campbed and Mrs

Johnson slept with the baby in the double bed. There was a chamber pot under the bed and a jug of water we shared at night, sucking from the spout. My nightmares disappeared miraculously. Fleur played truant from school a lot to keep Mrs Johnson company, and once while I was at school she and Mrs Johnson ate my chocolate ration. Before I came home she scored the one remaining piece into doll-sized squares, made a special chocolate wrapper and presented it to me. I was won over.

We invented new games of pretend. There was a wall alongside the village we called 'the wall that never ended'. In the summer evenings we picked handfuls of 'golden grass' and convinced ourselves it turned to gold for minutes at a time during the night. We played boarding school games. Fleur was a dashing tomboy type called Katie, while I was left with the role of Monica, a more neatly dressed second in command. She always managed to secure the roles and the names that I coveted in these games, but I stole them from her in my fantasies.

Mrs Johnson had a much smaller living room than Mrs Whittington and I was always underfoot, bobbing in her path while she fried chips on the coal range. Fleur ate everything put before her as usual while I wept into my mashed dumpling stew because it made me gag and I was hungry. Fleur used to fart a lot. Mrs Johnson would say, 'Do it out the door.' So after that Fleur opened the door and stuck out her bottom to fart. Mrs Johnson adored Fleur but I didn't feel entirely unsharing of her love. In the evenings she used to pore over her 'Spot the Ball' competition and listen to sentimental music on the wireless. 'This is a lovely way — to spend an evening,' she warbled. I thought it was. I felt safe, now that I was with Fleur, even if she was 'Jean'. We knitted dolls' garments out of stringy turquoise 'wool' that was actually cotton. Mrs Johnson marvelled at our 'oddness'. One thing she thought remarkable was our lack of interest in sugar. She had kissed the shopkeeper at the Naafi store for extra sugar, Fleur reported. We promised to bring her some of our sugar ration when we went home. We still thought Woodside Way was our home. We were waiting to go home.

We learned we were going to live in Chippenham in a very old house with an old man of eighty. Irene told us Mr Dolman was a grumpy old man, but I imagined myself becoming his friend. It didn't happen.

The house was dark and draped with heavy brown velvet curtains. The back kitchen was our territory because Irene did the cooking. It was very bare with a bare table in the middle. Fleur and I used to dance around the table singing a song I had made up called, 'Hee hee, jigajag.' We made walnut shell-boats, put love letters in them to Michael Glenny and Robin Manders, and set them sailing down the Avon River, which ran through a field at the back of the house.

The stairs were dark and steep and shook if you walked too fast. Our parents' bedroom was on the second floor and we used it as a living room too. It was winter and a clothes horse in front of the gas fire steamed our clothes dry. In the warm steamy atmosphere we revived Dreamland and composed chanting tunes to the poems in my *Child's Book of*

Lyrics. We also spent a lot of time inside Lear's *Book of Nonsense*. One of my favourite poems ended 'Get you gone, you drunken sot!'

Our bedroom was the attic, unfurnished, with a bare board floor. It was icy cold but we had a round kerosene heater that was left on low at night. We slept side by side on the floor with double bedding, but our two mattresses were of different heights and divided during the night. Fleur would sniff in a way that I hated. We conducted church services under the blankets with a torch, lying with our knees up, balancing hymnbook and Bible. Sometimes we did this while secretly chewing gum, which I and my new school friend, Joy, had cadged from American soldiers who were about the town. We had danced up to them and called, 'Any gum, chum?', as was the custom. Fleur was shocked at this but she chewed the long sticks of gum anyway. We stuck gum on the torch face and shone weird shapes on the sloping walls.

On New Year's Eve Fleur and I danced on the mattresses in our attic and sang Fleur's latest song, 'I've got a pain in my itchy belly, stitchy belly.'

One day Irene told me she was going to explain where babies came from. I laughed and said, 'I know all that.' Fleur and Mrs Johnson had discussed the subject in some lurid detail, which Fleur had passed on to me. Fleur had warned me that Irene might have another baby, which frightened me, but it didn't seem to be happening. One afternoon we looked in her chest of drawers and found something Fleur called a 'preventative', which was reassuring. I felt very grown up. I had turned nine.

Dreamland had begun as a boarding school called the Eagles' Nest, with classes named after birds. Fleur was in the Starlings and I was a Robin. At Chippenham Fleur added the Land of Happy Meetings, where we used to go from the Eagles' Nest at night, to meet Michael Glenny and Robin Manders. One cold Saturday Fleur and I accompanied the boys to a ball. Michael wore Robin Hood green and I was left having to dress Robin in something equally fetching. I gave him white satin pants. Fleur hooted and fell off the bed, rolling about the floor shrieking with laughter. I watched this performance, getting madder and madder until I finally sank my teeth in a pillowcase and wrenched, almost pulling my teeth out.

The news came that we were moving again. To Frant, a little Sussex village near Tunbridge Wells. Our belongings were packed up and our father began to move the boxes out into the car while Irene took us to the film *Song of Bernadette*. At the opening hospital scene I whispered, 'Are they all going to die?' Irene shook her head. It seemed to be about death just the same. We arrived home to find our rooms stripped. Only the double bed remained undisturbed. We were to spend our last night in it before our father came to collect us. Fleur and I were to sleep at one end, Irene at the other. She told us not to put our feet in her face. In the night I decided I had cancer of the throat like the man in the film. No one got very much sleep.

The house we moved to was rented by the Gains family, who sub-let the upstairs rooms to us. It was some distance from the village, surrounded by rolling meadows on one side and woods on the other.

Fleur gave me a present of a flower — a 'milkmaid' in a pot at the top of the meadow. A piece of wool attached to it ran down the bank to the pond below. She explained the wool would suck up water to feed the plant. It died, but quite slowly.

We were both enrolled at a private school in Tunbridge Wells, but Fleur soon deserted to the grammar school, leaving me to the mercy of the hard-eyed headmistress who stood over me daily while I choked down my school dinner, trying to sneak bits of inedible gristle up my sleeve. It had been better while Fleur was there — she had sometimes sat next to me and eaten what I couldn't.

One day Fleur had an argument with Irene and stomped off with her 'hiking staff' for a walk in the woods wearing Joan's old black coat, which she hated. It was late, then dark, and she hadn't returned. Neighbours began muttering about uncovered wells. The police were called but they were putting out a fire in the village. It was one of the more frightening days in my life. I fictionalised it in a 1959 story, *Look it Doesn't Bite.*

> *But when Ann got lost even her mother was frightened. The moment Lesley saw her mother frightened she went stiff all over as if she'd crack like toffee dropped in cold water if she tried to swim to the surface of her fear.*

When we left Frant we were going not 'home' to Woodside Way, but our piano and sideboard and loved walnut table

would be in the new house in Kent to welcome us. Our new home didn't disappoint us. Hatherley Road was a tree-lined street with grand houses and impressive gardens. The pavements were pink. Lanherne was three-storeyed, with three gable windows in the attic. A bricked courtyard led to an old coach-house without windows. The garden was pleasantly wild, with five pear trees, six apple trees and a rusty hammock to swing on. Our father had been working on the house, distempering the kitchen and repairing broken windows, while Irene scavenged for mats and curtain material, which was difficult in wartime. The worst of the raids were said to be over but the war went on and rationing didn't ease.

Our family occupied the ground floor; the other floors were let to a variety of tenants, but the huge garden was all ours. We were each given a piece of it. Against the bottom fence was the duck-run, like at Woodside Way.

Fleur and I lay in bed and plotted how to sneak into Germany and assassinate Hitler — they'd never suspect two harmless-looking children. We were at different schools again but of course we shared a bedroom and games and stories that we passed between each other until we succumbed to the enemy sleep. We had found an old piece of gas tubing to put between our beds and whisper down so that Irene wouldn't hear and come rapping on the door. Fleur tried whispering key words for a dream into my sleeping ear and then would wake me to check if it had worked.

I had 'the old nightmares' again when she visited me in Menton in 1980 and slept in the Katherine Mansfield room with me. While she was writing a poem in rhyming couplets for *Katherine* I was writing these lines:

But where did they travel from, these familiar horrors?
Were they caged in your head, crouched and watching,
Released by a small snore, to burrow across the pillow
And lodge in my left ear?

At Lanherne we invented a game called 'Imposter'. It arose out of my nightmares of Irene suddenly not being Irene at all, but an evil witch. One of us would try to tease the other into believing they were only pretending to be who they claimed to be. The idea was not to announce when you started to play the game; it could sneak in at any time. For instance, Fleur would suddenly make a mistake about one of my dolls' names, or call Irene 'Mum'. She was better at this game than I was. Her intentional slips would send me into a frenzy as I began to wonder if it was a game after all. I could quickly be reduced to a quivering wreck.

Mrs Curtis in one of the upstairs rooms was very pregnant and planned to have her baby at home. When she went into labour Fleur and I were sent overnight to stay with Margaret Shaw, our Ambulance Depot friend who had played 'lick tongues' with us when we were small. We had been her bridesmaids when she married Jack Smedley (I was nervous and had sworn, as I followed her down the aisle, that I would never get married) — and now she had two babies. We talked about having babies and sex, because of what was going on at home. She told us how exciting it was giving birth and

showed us her stretch-marks. She said she wanted to have lots more babies. I asked her how it was a man's sperm didn't come out in the ordinary way, when he peed, and how they knew to come out in the first place? She said it was because the man was so happy at being inside a woman. Suddenly it all made sense. It was the last thing I had wanted to understand about sex — something Fleur had been unable to tell me — and I thought I knew all I needed to know at last.

When the war ended we went camping and visited the seaside for the first time. All the way in the car we chanted, 'We're going to see the sea!' As if we hadn't sailed across the sea all the way from New Zealand. Each night at Minnis Bay we went to bed in the car. Our parents had an ex-army tent. We exchanged our usual stories and looked at the stars in the night sky. Fleur told me about Rutherford splitting the atom and I looked up into the sky again and got very scared that the world would end.

We developed a taste for sleeping outdoors. Our front bedroom at Lanherne was let for the summer to a tenant and our father cleared a space in the bicycle shed big enough for our double bed and bookshelves. He made a canvas drop curtain for when it rained. Fleur would frighten me with tales of leprosy. She would turn her white blob of a face to me in the dusk of the bicycle shed and whisper that she was a leper. 'Look at my white skin!' Another time she told me that if I got leprosy I would be banished to an island and wouldn't see my family ever again. When I pleaded she conceded, 'Well, maybe Mummy will be allowed to go and look at you through a grating and say Uurgh!'

Because Fleur was so publicly clever, I deduced that my parents thought I was dim, like my friend Ann. Fleur was going to be a doctor or scientist. 'You can be a masseuse,' they said to me. I knew I wasn't as stupid as they seemed to believe — I had come top of the preliminary intelligence test at school — but that didn't stop me deliberately ignoring the maths paper of the eleven plus exam so as to go with Ann to the secondary modern school at the bottom of our road. Fleur's grammar school, where we went to sit the exam, was a dark scary place, unlike the bright friendly 'modern school'. I told myself I would redeem my pride later with works of literary genius. I was tricked — Irene managed to enrol me at the convent up the road, where I made a new friend nearly as good as Fleur at imaginary games — and began to have nightmares about Hell.

Fleur has since apologised more than once for 'the things I did to you'. In fact, I can see from this distance that it could be irritating having a silly little sister, quavering with ludicrous fears. And how else did I drive her crazy? I'm sure I did.

In 1947 we boarded the SS *Arawa* for New Zealand, our mythical birthplace. I couldn't remember much more of it than sinister knots in a timber wall beside my cot, the miraculous taste of passionfruit, Maori children from my father's school chasing after us to give us brown-skinned dolls

with grass skirts. Nevertheless it had loomed like a ghostly backdrop behind our English wartime years. Friends had asked us, 'Do all New Zealanders have silly little noses like yours?' The trip back seemed just another journey to just another 'home', but in fact this was to be the biggest displacement we had suffered. Fleur was journeying ahead of me in other ways. On the ship we both developed a crush on a dark handsome steward, Louis, but Fleur's crush was somehow more important than mine. My shipboard friend Fiona and I were allowed to watch while they kissed chastely on the deck. (We have since worked out he was certainly gay.)

All my young life I had worn Fleur's hand-me-down clothes and I can see at this remove that she handed down more than coats and dresses. I watched and followed, two steps behind. In Wellington for the first time the roles sometimes reversed. I handed on to her my navy convent uniform because it was what she needed for Wellington Girls, while Irene sewed for me a royal blue coat (not quite the right shade) for Queen Margaret College. Different schools had become the norm for us. I published my first two novels before Fleur published her first volume of poetry. If she didn't like this she didn't let me know. I was only relieved to have an achievement to put up against her school dux and university classics prizes.

I am failing to convey how much pleasure and richness there was in being a sister, Fleur's sister, as I grew. Her head was seething with ideas as vivid as my own; some of them frightened me, but I was eager to share them all. She might have encouraged my fears with one hand, but she allayed them with the other. I turned trustingly to her for advice and for comfort. Our parents were the 'Growns' — there were things we knew we could never share with them, things they could never understand. We were conspirators in the war game of life, uniquely close. She was my big sister, a manipulative tease, but she was also my protector and, when necessary, a surrogate mother. When, at thirteen, I told Irene there was a tight band squeezing my forehead, she dismissed it as a headache. I had had headaches — I knew this was different, possibly terminal. Fleur explained kindly that it was 'because you just started your periods'. (This even though she was resentful at not having yet started her own.) I relaxed at once into her explanation and my headband began to untie itself.

We both sprouted adolescent spots but mine were much worse than Fleur's. I developed regular sties on my eyes and had to wear an ugly eye patch. I needed glasses in my fifth form year while Fleur went prettily without. She was scathing about how much sleep I needed — 'What will you do when you grow up?' But when I fell asleep reading in bed she would take my glasses off and fold them carefully.

We had bedrooms of our own in our Kauri Street house in Miramar, although we shared a tent on our lawn during the polio epidemic. Sometimes we would go for a canter in the dusk, talking as we ran. Fleur called this 'going for a beetle' because of the insects which flew into our faces from the night air.

When, in 1963, Fleur left for England on an Italian boat I didn't believe that she would return only as a visitor. She became words on air letter forms, often nearly illegible, always interesting. I felt for her, all 'by herself' away from 'home'. In fact she had made England her home again, finding a place to live in East Finchley with the fortuitous help of Irene, who happened to be there on holiday at the right time. I didn't hear Fleur's voice again until at least ten years later, when we received a planned telephone call at Irene's house — toll calls were rare and expensive in those days. She sounded different, very English. When I came off the telephone and was asked by the assembled family, 'What did she say?' I was still in a state of shock and muttered, 'I don't know.' In 1975 she returned to New Zealand for the first time. I was the first to catch sight of her at the airport. I was convinced her mouth had changed shape but within minutes her features had reassembled into Fleur, my sister.

In East Finchley we go for brisk evening walks to Cherry Tree Wood, looking out for housemartins swooping in the dusk. We go home and listen to *A Book At Bedtime* holding our identical transistor radios to one ear as we pass each other on the landing preparing for bed. Today we don't tell each other stories at bedtime or compose ritual verses to chant in unison. We write our fiction and poems apart from one another, for more public attention. But we read each other's work eagerly, seeing things the ordinary reader might miss. We take pleasure in each other's successes. Fleur might point out that I have the Robinson ankles but she would never be cruel about my writing.

Not everything needs to be spelled out between us. I've noticed how on occasion we have been invaded by an identical thought or idea at nearly the same time. The 'chain ghost' who lived in the lavatory we invented quite independently of each other as children, just as we always knew or imagined that there was water under the house, if you took a spade and dug. We both shared the same horror of dying, not because death itself frightened us but because 'Mummy and Daddy would be so sad'. It has felt at times as if our genes were thinking for us, as if some of our brain cells were linked.

At the same time we are enormously different and resent being confused. It was disturbing to find, when we visited Writers' Week in Dunedin that we wore similar colours and clothes and marched around the streets nearly in step. (I've learned to walk faster.) Sometimes, listening to a tape of myself I catch an intonation that is Fleur — where did that come from? I'm a New Zealander, who enjoys terakihi, while she is now a Londoner who dines on mackerel. She goes to church, I don't, except with Fleur on Christmas Eve (I think of our church services under the bedclothes). She is poet, I am novelist. Sometimes in her company in London I've slipped and introduced myself as Marilyn Adcock.

The children we were in the bicycle shed of Lanherne would be shocked and astonished to meet us suddenly now. There have been so many twists and turns in our lives. We have had, in some ways, shocking lives, complex lives, certainly not ordinary or untroubled. Six marriages between us. We have veered between farce and tragedy but never come off the rails. We are strong women, as we were strong, loved children. Fleur and I both believe we know the best way of doing things, and sometimes even today this will lead to an argument. When I stand up for myself now, a baffled look of surprise floats onto her face. I have forgotten to be her little sister.

Fleur and I travelled to Sidcup by train more recently, taking a packed lunch and hot Caro in a thermos flask. We had been warned that Lanherne had been pulled down and the road altered to allow the building of council houses. We found one of our pear trees — the second one of five, which I thought of as mine — still standing by the side of the new road. It was something to marvel at. We sat down on the pavement and began to have our picnic. It was a grey day. A woman came down the road and looked surprised. She asked if we would like to come inside and have a cup of tea with our picnic. We explained why we would prefer to stay under the pear tree and she understood. She remembered Lanherne. There are small ways of being happy. Fleur and I have taught each other some of them.

FLEUR ADCOCK

Bluebell Seasons

Fleur Adcock OBE was born in Auckland, New Zealand, in 1934, but spent a wartime childhood in England. Since 1963 she has made her home in north London and held fellowships in Newcastle, Durham, the Lake District and also in Adelaide, Australia. Her numerous collections of poetry include *Selected Poems,* which won the New Zealand Book Award for poetry in 1984 and *The Incident Book* (1986). Her latest volume is *Time-Zones* (1991). She has translated poems from medieval Latin, including 'The Virgin and the Nightingale', and also collections of contemporary Romanian poetry. She edited *The Faber Book of Twentieth Century Women's Poetry* and co-edited *The Oxford Book of Creatures* (1995).

'My sister.' Imagine not being able to use that phrase — casually, automatically, proudly, affectionately, or with irritation; imagine being a female person and having no sister. Think of the desolation, the gap. I can't. Or rather, I can dimly and shudderingly imagine losing the sister I have, but never to have had one at all would make me an inconceivably different person. When I hear another woman say 'my sister' some kind of contented click registers itself in my mind: good, she's got one too; she's one of the sisterhood of sisters. My mother, nieces and grandchildren all have sisters; that seems normal. Most normal of all, my own experience tells me, is to have just one sister. And yet to be one of two sisters accounts for some of the most violent, passionate and savage emotions a young human being is capable of.

I didn't always have a sister. She always had me, but I was twenty-one months old (exactly) before I had her — too young for consoling explanations about how we were both loved equally, and far too young to be told or to understand that the arrival of a second child so soon after the first had not been the plan. She was an accident! What a weapon that would have been, had I possessed it and been capable of deploying it! But, looking back, it would have been a rubber sword; our parents showed no sign of being anything but overwhelmingly delighted with their little mistake.

Not long ago I saw in the street an archetypal scene: a small boy of about three bent over a pushchair hugging his baby brother in a sadistically fierce embrace and wearing a

wide, false grin — loving him to death, as it were. I felt for them both: the younger child's unease, the older one's despair. No rejection in later life is ever quite so devastating as the first. In the occasional vicissitudes of our wartime childhood, when for good reasons we were separated from our parents, I never suffered as Marilyn did. To her it must have seemed, when, aged four and six, we were sent away from the Blitz to stay with relatives, that Mummy and Daddy no longer wanted her. Apart from being older and better able to accept their explanations, I was more philosophical. Parental changes of heart were no novelty to me; after all, if they had loved me as much as they initially made out they would not have replaced me. Obviously I had not come up to their expectations — a disappointment which I compounded by being horrible to Marilyn and consequently harder to love. The world is full of first-born children behaving badly to their younger rivals. I was a particularly beastly example.

And yet I loved her — of course I did. She was my great comfort and closest companion; whenever we went somewhere new it was us against the world, just as, in the family circle, it was us against the grown-ups. She was a lovable child, a sweet little blonde, blue-eyed thing who invited protective feelings. The fact that she also invited bullying was beyond my control; everyone needs someone to bully, just as they need someone to love. In our later childhood Marilyn now and then took up with friends who were younger or more dim-witted than herself, and could be dominated or impressed. (I don't suggest that she bullied them.) My own need for pliable subordinates was fulfilled by her, until we reached a point when the age difference became less significant; I chose friends who were my equals.

Enough analysis; now for some chronology. I was born on 10 February 1934, when my father was teaching at Graham's Beach on the Manukau Harbour. When Marilyn was born on 10 November 1935 we had already spent nearly a year at Kuaotunu in the Coromandel Peninsula, and were to be there for another year. It is the first place I remember, and I have no conscious recollection of a world without Marilyn in it — in all my memories of Kuaotunu (watering the garden with my little red watering can, drawing a 'face' on the blackboard which turned out not to be a face at all, sitting in the kitchen with our mother and 'Jammy Jean' who came to help her for a while after the birth) the baby was already there, as a vague presence. I have no clear vision of her until 1937, when we moved to Palmerston North. There she materialises as a little figure sitting in the sandpit. I ran into the house calling 'Mummy, Baby's eating sand!' (Did I add 'again'?) As so often, my motives seem ambiguous: was I protecting her infant digestion, or showing off my superior common sense? Perhaps eating sand was one of the few interesting things she did, in my view. We were still separate units: she was 'Baby', I was a girl.

By the time we left for England in June 1939 my sister had become a playmate. If she could not reach my imaginative level, I was happy to descend to hers. At our grandmother's house in Drury, the very night before we sailed, we decided to sit our dolls on the potty. Unfortunately we had already sat

on it ourselves. The furious adult reactions to our pee-soaked dolls were matched by our own howls on being told that the soggy objects would have to be left behind. My favourite doll, Margaret, was reprieved, though — perhaps I had taken care not to dunk her too deeply?

Margaret was named after the little princess, Margaret Rose, one of another pair of sisters. The royal duo probably had more of an influence on my mother, as models for her own small daughters, than she would be willing to acknowledge now that her tastes have progressed so far beyond those of 1930s popular culture. Marilyn was christened Marilyn Rose, although, like the princess, she later abolished the second element (just as I officially discarded the unwelcome first name which originally came before Fleur on my birth certificate. Our family is beset by problems over names.)

Like many sisters we were often dressed alike. In a studio photograph taken when we were about four and two we are wearing identical tussore silk or crêpe-de-Chine dresses, lovingly smocked and embroidered by our mother; we are gazing at a Mickey Mouse the photographer has placed in Marilyn's hand. She looks interested; I look meekly co-operative, or indeed smug. Naturally it is she who has been given the toy, but this time it is to keep her still, and not just because she is so cute. At least she is not wearing the little anxious frown she so often has in photographs; you would think, from her image in later posed studies, that she found the world an alarming place. When she was seven or eight, for example, we acted as bridesmaids for a family friend and were photographed in our long red velvet dresses; Marilyn's worried face shows what a terrifying responsibility she found it all, whereas I revelled in my importance. Photographs can lie, of course; which of us was basically the more timid varied from time to time over the years.

We arrived in England in September 1939, in nice time for the war. This was, needless to say, not the object (our father had long been planning to do his PhD in London) but, being adventurous New Zealanders, he and our mother stayed for the duration. They did not wish to subject us to any risks, though, and this and other factors resulted in a good deal of moving around. At first, while we lived in Sidcup, they both worked in the Civil Defence Ambulance Service; Marilyn and I were subjected to a few babysitters, who helped to unify us as a partnership. I went to two schools (the first one soon closed) while Marilyn stayed at home playing school.

From this point onwards her memories run parallel to mine, and are reliable. She has a brilliant memory. Like mine, it dates back to the age of two, but from then on I have the impression that she remembers most of what I do and more besides, although perhaps I have retained different episodes, such as the time in Sidcup when we had just been taught to knit, and a tactless visitor, seduced by Marilyn's innocent blue eyes, said *her* knitting was better than mine. This outraged my sense of justice and logic: I might be a pushy, objectionable child, but I hadn't dropped any stitches.

Early in 1940, when the Blitz got going properly, we were sent off to Scalford in Leicestershire to stay with 'Uncle George' (our father's second-cousin-by-marriage), his wife

'Auntie Eva', and their two daughters (more sisters) on their farm. Water came from the pump, heat from the coal range, lighting from gas downstairs and candles in the bedrooms. Nothing except the separator for the dairy was mechanised; milking was by hand, horses pulled the plough and the market-cart. It was a rural idyll. We went to the village school together (although Marilyn was technically too young) and to Sunday School, and roamed around the fields and farmyards. For nine months we were, as I recall it, perfectly happy. Our parents visited when they could, and we sent them letters (or in Marilyn's case pictures). I began writing poems.

When I was nearly seven our mother took us away to live with her, first at lodgings in Salfords, Surrey, and then in a small rented house in nearby Outwood, surrounded by woods. I went to my sixth school (there had been one in New Zealand before we left); Marilyn should have gone too, but for weeks she was at home with whooping cough, to my indignation. I was being teased at school and could have done with an ally. As revenge (I can only suppose) I teased her; I came home one day with a smear of black grease on my leg, from some forgotten encounter, and when she asked about it I said I hadn't been to school but to work in a bicycle shop. For a few minutes she believed me. Power! She was not always so gullible, but we had been brought up to tell the truth, a habit which still persists, and lies threw us into confusion.

The cruellest trick I ever played on her (which I later obliterated from my memory, although it is seared on hers) was to tell her that her doll Pixie Ann had not always been a doll — 'She was a little girl once, but her father shot her and had her stuffed.' This struck at her trust in both dolls and fathers. I cringe to think of it. (The poor child's faith in what had been her other basic certainty was undermined when we saw a film about some children whose mother turned into a witch; for months her nightmare was that ours might.)

Marilyn was always the doll-lover. I lost interest in playing with mine fairly early — but not before I had conned her into swapping round the two almost identical dolls we had received for Christmas 1940, so that I got the one with real eyelashes. I had three: Margaret from New Zealand, Joan with the eyelashes, and Gwen, made by our mother. I also had a furry dog, Bobbie, whom I took to bed and cuddled almost to disintegration. Marilyn's equivalent dog remained pristine, but her dolls were greatly cuddled, and their numbers kept growing; she was given extra ones because they were what she liked as presents; and she pressed any doll-like object into service as a member of her expanding family: a pottery gnome or a dangerously temporary figure made from plasticine would join the circle ranged around her bed at night or the ranks lined up on the floor for lessons.

My dolls, by contrast, went to boarding school — that is, into a suitcase, to be brought out on rare occasions. This kept them in good condition; they survive, and are now living in Marilyn's house to replace hers, which, through no fault of her own, she lost in adult life. What I liked doing for my dolls was making clothes; I designed smart little outfits for them, carefully stitched out of scraps of old material: fur-lined slippers, embroidered bonnets and jackets, a beaded veil.

But I've jumped ahead. From Outwood we moved in the summer of 1941 to a house of our own a few miles away, between Salfords and Earlswood. The street was called Woodside Way, and there were still woods at the end of it, with a field beside them: rural suburbia, as it were. We stayed for three years, the longest we lived anywhere in England. Marilyn and I had time to make friends, both locally and at school, but still spent a good deal of time together. We formed a club called 'Secret Exploring Indians', with me as the chief — a position that she seemed to agree was mine by a law of nature. Often we roamed in the woods and on the common, picking bluebells or primroses, climbing trees (well, I climbed them — her function was to stand below looking alarmed at my daring), looking for tadpoles, and playing out fantasies. Such freedom is no longer available to English children, now that parents are so terrified of murderers and child abusers, but those were more innocent days. All our mother had to worry about was an occasional air raid: we were told to run home at once if the siren sounded.

My conscience compels me to mention, once again, the darker side of our relationship: my too often expressed scorn for Marilyn's babyishness. She was a nervous child (to use our mother's relatively tactful adjective — my contemptuous word was 'scared') and given to bizarre imaginings. I could share realistic fears (strange dogs) and a few less rational ones; I was occasionally known to get the horrors after reading ghost stories, but I'd have thought it beneath me to ask for adult comfort. Marilyn had no such inhibition. Just as I was getting to sleep in our shared bedroom I might be annoyed by her plaintive wail: 'Mu-ummy! I'm frightened!'

Snakes were her particular phobia: was there an adder in the bed? Was that long ridge in the blankets a boa constrictor? Ghosts and ghouls and nameless hauntings also featured in her night terrors. I played on this by telling her spooky stories, and chanting an atmospheric little ditty which began 'All round the house is the jet-black night . . .'

I could understand genuine nightmares, though. We both had a rich dream life. I can remember in detail several vivid dreams of mine from those years, and I even partook in a couple of hers, after she had related them to me. One was the nightmare about things changing their size — the 'big and little' experience. The other centred on the word 'buttoning', which had taken on inexplicably sinister overtones: 'Look! It's *buttoning*!'

One of my own most unforgettable dreams was about Marilyn: she was kneeling on a huge birthday cake, with her legs and feet somehow splayed sideways to support her; she said this position was a 'Bluebell Dance'. I reacted with my usual scorn — '*That*'s not a bluebell dance!' — and was then suddenly flooded with a sense of such overpowering remorse and tenderness towards her that I can feel it still. Tears come to my eyes when I think of it: poor little Marilyn doing her special act and being despised for it. It epitomized all that she had suffered at my hands. For years I could sometimes (but not often enough) control my irritation with her by summoning up this dream.

Our school was St John's in Earlswood: a church school, with boys and girls segregated in separate classes and a high wall between the two playgrounds. We went there on the bus

or, in summer, on foot across the common, at first with older kids and later alone. I liked it well enough and made good progress, being promoted to a higher class halfway through one year so that from then on I was always a year ahead of my contemporaries. Marilyn was in the infants' when we began — I used to meet her at playtime, in her little brown pixie-hood if it was cold, and we'd play together. Later, when she arrived in the junior school, for some reason she became unhappy, and our parents eventually decided to transfer her to a small private school, St Hilda's. After this we were very seldom at the same school together (the exceptions being two brief spells when we were in transit). Three out of her six subsequent schools were private ones, whereas I always stayed in the state system, apart from a week or so with her at a horrible little school in Tunbridge Wells when I was eleven, before arrangements had been made for me at the Girls' Grammar.

I suppose this separation created some kind of distinction between us: I was the academic one, briskly getting on with things; she was the delicate flower in need of protection (not that any school provides that!). But this is a false simplification, and in any case we both suffered equal anxiety every time we confronted new schools. One clear difference between us, though, was that I was better at exams, which I actually rather enjoyed, and she better at artistic or musical activities. We both had ballet lessons, but I dropped out while she continued, a graceful little figure in her tutu in one of the few wartime photographs; later we both learned to play the violin, but I gave it up at fourteen to concentrate on School Certificate, whereas she played until quite recently.

Our peaceful, settled spell in Woodside Way was ended in 1944 by the doodlebugs, which came uncomfortably close. We had to move on, first to Leicestershire again for a few blissful weeks and then to Wiltshire, where our mother was helping to run an agricultural camp for people who spent working holidays getting the harvest in. (Our father, as always, was at the Civil Defence Depot in Sidcup, with only every third weekend free to visit us.) Marilyn and I were boarded out with two families in adjacent tiny cottages near Corsham. Conditions were delightfully primitive — no running water nearer than the communal village tap, and not too much attention to hygiene, education, or the other respectable standards we had been brought up with. When it turned out that the father in Marilyn's household was a bit of a drunk she moved into mine. We shared the only bedroom with Mrs J. and her toddler (Mr J. was away in the army), our narrow beds crammed against the walls; I can still see Marilyn huddled under the blankets biting her nails.

This was understandable. Much as we enjoyed our taste of unsupervised licence to be grubby little hoydens, it was more fun for me than for Marilyn, who was still Mummy's girl at heart. Also she had to go to school every day; I didn't. Mrs J. liked having me at home to keep her company; often she set the clock extravagantly fast or slow, so that I either missed the bus to my terrifying new co-educational school in Chippenham or thought I had, when it failed to turn up half an hour early. After Marilyn had set out across the fields to her village school I'd come back for a day of idleness. This involved me in a conspiracy against my poor sister, whom I was not supposed to tell, although she sometimes guessed.

Alongside this unpleasant deception our usual principles of loyalty and honesty prevailed. For Marilyn's ninth birthday in November I made a set of doll's furniture (a matchbox chest of drawers, cardboard armchairs covered with fabric). Until it was finished it stood on the mantelpiece draped with a large handkerchief. I made her swear not to look, and she didn't. The fact that I could trust her and she be trustworthy baffled Mrs J.

Time stretches in retrospect, but it can have been only a couple of months before certain indications (such as the lice in our hair and the sores on our feet) alerted our mother to the state of things, and she whisked us away to live with her in Chippenham; Marilyn went to another school, I attended mine more consistently. After that it was Christmas — dark and frosty and wonderful, with carol singing in the streets and a cosy glow in the attic room where Marilyn and I slept. After that we moved to lodgings in a cottage in Frant, on the Kent–Sussex border near Tunbridge Wells. Just before dusk one evening I got thoroughly lost in the woods across the road, which extended for miles, and trudged wearily home after dark to find Marilyn and our landlady's young daughter sitting on the kitchen table sobbing on each other's necks because I must be dead.

It was 1945, and the war was edging towards its end. Our father was appointed regional organiser in Kent for the WEA (Workers' Educational Association), and bought a large, tall Victorian house in Sidcup with a coach-house and stables and a huge garden. We lived mostly on the ground floor; the two upper floors were filled with an interestingly unpredictable population of tenants. Something like settled normality returned to our lives. We were at different schools, as was now usual — I at the Girls' Grammar, Marilyn at the local primary school and then, after she failed the eleven-plus examination for grammar school entry (deliberately, she says, although the idea of anyone wilfully failing an examination still shocks me), at the convent I had attended in 1939. We each made friends of our own; and fought less; the disgraceful episodes when I bit her, or threw a fork at her (it missed) belong to an earlier period.

We had both become writers, in an intermittent fashion, and filled notebooks with stories and poems when we were in the mood. Another imaginative outlet, and one which held us together, was storytelling, or regaling each other with episodes of the latest news from a shared fantasy world we had invented. It was called Dreamland, and centred on a boarding school where each of us had a circle of imaginary friends and got up to wilder larks and pranks than those we read about in school stories: not just midnight feasts in the dorm, but all-night jamborees in the woods. (At Corsham our drooling accounts of rabbits roasted over a campfire had been so graphic that Mrs J. took them as a hint and managed to get a real rabbit from the butcher.)

I also extemporised stories based on the characters in Richmal Crompton's books to entertain Marilyn. At one point I actually made money out of this, having persuaded her to pay me a farthing a time for William stories, but before I'd

made more than a few pence I relented; after all, I enjoyed the telling as much as she the listening — what came into my head after the ritual opening 'William and Ginger were walking along the road' was always as much a surprise to me as to her.

Another thing we did together was singing. She was the real singer, having a better voice, but it was fun to make up songs and silly jingles, or to go through the repertoire of carols we knew by heart. Years later, when we were both middle-aged and she was Katherine Mansfield Fellow in Menton, we marched through Ventimiglia together singing *La Normandie*; its deliciously melancholy air and nostalgic sentiments expressed perfectly the yearning for past scenes which has been such a dominating emotion of our lives.

Nostalgia really came into its own when, in 1947, we had to leave England and try to become New Zealanders again. Leaving was agonising; travelling on the SS *Arawa* was a thing in itself, memorable but separate; arriving felt unreal. For a while we drifted around grandparents' houses in Drury and Papatoetoe, until things were settled in Wellington, where our father had a job at the university but at first nowhere to live. Marilyn and I became 'the girls', our parents' daughters, skinny children with underfed frames (wartime rationing — 'legs like pea-sticks' someone said). Inside we were explosive capsules of memories. The English ones had to remain sealed, except in our endless, obsessive conversations about what we had left behind, but Drury, where our maternal grandmother still lived with her son Len and his family, was itself part of the memory-pack; we wandered around the village and along the creek, wallowing in flashbacks to 1939, and slept in the room where we had dunked the dolls.

Our father's parents now lived in Papatoetoe. When it was their turn to have us we slept in a bach at the back of the house stored with the overflow of their and our father's possessions — old *School Journals* from his teaching days, quaint, mouldering English magazines (*Titbits*, featuring the feeble jokes which so appealed to our grandfather's odd sense of humour). We were not, perhaps, ideal grandchildren. One day when our parents had gone out for the afternoon Grandma Adcock fell and broke her wrist. Grandpa went to the hospital with her, leaving us to transmit this distressing piece of news. The responsibility was too much for our silly young nerves. We practised solemn expressions, but when we heard the bus stopping a short distance along the road, and set out to meet our mother and father, we found our faces breaking into involuntary smiles. They smiled back, looking pleased. This was all wrong, but try as we might to control ourselves our idiotic grins only widened. We lapsed into hysterical giggles; they advanced happily towards us, waiting to hear the joke. Finally, almost speechless, we managed to force out some words: 'Grandma . . .' Yes? 'Grandma's broken her wrist.' Instantly their smiles vanished — and so, far too late, did ours.

Eventually the long weeks in each other's constant company came to an end. Our self-absorbed idleness was over, and we were forced to confront the necessity of becoming New Zealanders instead of merely observing the species from outside, like not particularly sympathetic anthropologists. In Wellington I was enrolled, aged thirteen, at my thirteenth school, and Marilyn, aged eleven, at her eleventh. Mine was Wellington Girls' College, hers Queen Margaret's (a private school which catered for both primary and secondary levels); for each of us it was, thank God, the last.

At some point in my early teens the system of strict justice with which we were treated broke down, or so I saw it: suddenly Marilyn began to receive the same amount of pocket money as I did, and was allowed to stay up until the same hour at night. 'Not fair — when I was twelve I got only two shillings!' I'd complain in vain, as the privileges of my two years' seniority melted away. Evidently our parents now found it easier to see us as equals rather than at different stages on a parallel track. In most ways we had always, of course, been treated equally: when we had new clothes they were similar, if in different colours, and chosen for us or inflicted without our consent (like the brown tweed 'costumes', inherited from another pair of sisters, with which we arrived from England; our hatred of these was increased by the fact that the skirts were too long, our mother having foreseen the 'New Look' which hit New Zealand only later). It was a relief when we were at last allowed to choose our own clothes.

We moved separately into adolescence, with different friends and interests. I was a swot, compulsively immersed in books. I also allowed myself to be socialised, up to a point: as we lived in Miramar, miles from our schools, we were sent to Bible class at the local Presbyterian church to 'make friends'

(= meet boys), and joined the youth club for such innocent activities as table tennis, chess and square dancing. Marilyn endured this for a year or two and then dropped out; I, seeing some advantages in knowing a few boys, continued. What she did when not in my company I scarcely knew or noticed; but we still spent time together at weekends and during the holidays, particularly at Paremata, where we had a boatshed, or on family trips up the North Island; and we shared the usual teenage agonies over our appearance. I thought I was too thin, she thought she was too fat. On one journey we sat in the back of the car bewailing the shape of our arms. 'Look at my fat arm — ugh!' moaned Marilyn. 'Look at my horrible skinny one!' I groaned. 'Nonsense, they're both exactly the same,' said a brisk parental voice from the front seat. 'It's just that Fleur's are longer.'

Marilyn was a late developer as far as looks were concerned (although physically more advanced in other ways). It has to be admitted that there was a grain of truth in her complaints about plump arms, and her well-rounded, although far from podgy, teenage features effectively concealed the excellent bone structure which was to be such an asset in later years. Also she was short-sighted (as I became in my thirties) and had to wear glasses from the age of fifteen. (Not long ago someone who had not known us in our youth saw some photographs from that period, and without having time to reflect on the implications said, 'Oh, Fleur was the pretty one *then*!') Sometimes on my way home from school I'd see her at the tram stop, in her royal blue QMC uniform and singularly unbecoming beret, gazing dreamily into space.

She had a close friend, a vague and rather moon-faced girl who was a passive admirer of Marilyn's superior intelligence and a partner in her imaginative schemes. After they left school this poor young woman developed a chronic mental illness and was committed to an institution, taking a huge bundle of their shared memories out of Marilyn's reach as far as future reminiscing was concerned.

When I was eighteen I got married. Naturally my sister was my bridesmaid. She has never forgiven me for the dress she was forced to wear (pale blue taffeta with a rolled boat neckline) which for some reason she loathed. I was not responsible for the dress — or indeed for my own, a prim affair with a little round collar and buttons up to the neck, which I thought far too meek and childlike for a bride; the dressmaker had designed them, with our mother's connivance. Really we were both still children. In the eyes of the world, though, I was a married woman (and also a busy student in my second year at university), while Marilyn was a schoolgirl living at home. I was pleased to see her when we met, but we didn't seek each other out.

Life went on. I finished my BA and had a baby. Marilyn was by now a student herself, with boyfriends — proper ones, as opposed to the rather gormless admirer with the embarrassing surname who had hung around her while she was still at school. The most serious boyfriend, Richard, was a charming young man whom we all liked — he helped Alistair to paint our bedroom, and used to visit our Adcock grandparents, who had moved to Wellington. Unfortunately our parents were about to travel to America on a sabbatical, and got into a Victorian panic at the idea of leaving the ardent young couple unsupervised. They plotted to send Marilyn away to England on a working holiday. On board the *Mataroa* she met Harry Duckworth, saw him nine months later in London, broke off her engagement to Richard and married him. She was nineteen.

It was two years before I saw her again. Early in 1956 she and Harry decided that it would be wiser for their baby to be born in New Zealand. Our first meeting happened to be at a party. She was six months pregnant, but showing no sign of it, in her slim, elegant, long dress. Was this sophisticated vision of loveliness truly my little sister? She was actually wearing eye shadow, something which it had never occurred to me even to contemplate (she had to instruct me in its use). Rapid readjustments took place. And as for the shock, a year or two later, when she suddenly announced that she was having a novel published . . .

But perhaps I should leave us there, both temporarily moored in youthful marriages which would not last. Why did we do it? Neither of us was pregnant (nothing so scandalous). Marilyn said later she thought she'd better grab this chance in case no one else ever asked her — which, as Harry's proposal had followed fast on the heels of another, seemed unlikely. In my case, I didn't want Alistair to fall into the hands of one of his older and more glamorous girlfriends, who had not yet given up hopes of him. But in retrospect I blame the fifties, with their wedding-culture, their assumption that marriage was the only destiny for a woman. No one was going to take us seriously until we had proved that we were adults (which

of course we weren't), and acquiring a husband seemed a short cut to this status; as married women we could get away from the parental nest and kid ourselves that we were leading independent lives.

Genuine independence came soon enough, for both of us. The procession of our emotional turmoils — divorces, love affairs, more marriages, more divorces, shifts and separations, agonies and transformations — had scarcely begun. They are not my subject here, except as they affected our relationship with each other (and even there certain doors will remain firmly locked). Melodrama and black comedy have featured abundantly in our lives, in shifting proportions; what feels like a dramatic crisis of Sophoclean dimensions often turns out, in retrospect, to have been more in the nature of farce. I had my quota of ups and downs, which there is no way of measuring, but when I look at the simple statistics from a purely official point of view — that of the Registrar of Births, Deaths and Marriages — Marilyn comes out on top: she had twice as many children and husbands as I did (four of each, as opposed to my two), and also had to endure being widowed, when her third husband died suddenly of a heart attack.

It happened on a Sunday in 1978. I was in England, where I'd been living for years, and our mother was also there, visiting me. Instead of disturbing us in the middle of the night Marilyn waited until it was Sunday morning in London, and then I picked up the telephone beside my bed to hear a small, stunned voice say, 'Dan died this afternoon.' I was with a kind man, fairly new in my life; we were happy. Somehow I managed to grasp and believe the dreadful message, and to talk to Marilyn, and to get over my storm of weeping; but throughout it all another voice inside my head was saying, 'Can we never both be happy at the same time?' I felt a wave of superstitious guilt, as if I'd snatched away her share of some rationed commodity.

The system of fair shares and exactly equal treatment which had been applied to us in childhood was probably not a very good preparation for adult life; it gave us, or at least me, false expectations of other domestic relationships, such as marriage. If Alistair spent an hour in the pub after work several times a week, when was I going to get my turn? I had to admit that he was admirably generous about taking turns over cooking and, once we had a baby, child-minding, but I couldn't help feeling there was some imbalance in the set-up. Fortunately by the time I encountered more typical examples of the Kiwi male I was reconciled to a certain amount of injustice, but at least one relationship foundered on my refusal to be a doormat.

In relation to Marilyn it was a long time before I weaned myself of the habit of making comparative lists. I managed, with difficulty, not to envy her the two extra children (and as for the husbands, although I was pleased to see her happy with Dan and, later, John, marriage was by then the last thing I'd have wanted for myself). In our literary careers she 'got ahead of me' for a while, but we have operated in different fields — she in New Zealand, with fiction, and I mostly in England, with poetry — and there is no real element of competition. If we were to tot up the number of titles published and the number of international conferences attended it might well come out roughly equal, but who cares? The important thing

is that, because we lead fairly similar professional lives, we understand each other's needs and problems. Our mother once said, in a moment of despair at her volatile daughters, 'I wish you'd both married farmers and settled down in the country.' What if we had? What if *one* of us had, and the other one had been left with nothing to say to her?

Seeing that we are now so in tune with each other and share so many interests, I thought I might permit myself to draw up a short checklist of our differences, at this relatively calm point in our lives. It turned out not to be very short at all. To begin with the trivial, I smoke; she never has. She eats sweets; I never do except when caught in a non-smoking dilemma. I drive a car; she doesn't. I spent years of my youth studying, finally graduated with an MA in classics, and still enjoy a certain amount of research and translating from foreign languages; she dropped out of university at an early stage and confined herself to writing — and reading — instead. She watches television and keeps up with popular culture; I am a radio addict, devoted to the BBC, and listen to hours of news and classical music (although she is more musically talented as a performer). I am keen on gardening, natural history, wildlife and bird-watching — the high point of my year is the English spring, when the bulbs come up in my garden and the bluetits and robins make their nests; she quite likes birds but hates gardening, and would never, as I did, fall in love with a spider which had made a web in the pantry window and fling aphids into its clutches when it ran short of flies. (But she does love English wild flowers, and is frustrated that she never gets to England at bluebell time.)

Physically we are said to resemble each other (which used to bewilder us in our teens — how could anyone possibly guess that two such different people were related, we asked each other, after a shopkeeper who didn't even know us had remarked, 'Your sister was in here a minute ago.'). She, however, is the more petite, feminine version of the family type; she goes to hairdressers, and wears long droopy skirts. I live mostly in casual clothes, trousers and trainers. Our daily patterns differ: I like mornings, and do my best work before lunch; her sleep disorder means that she seldom sees a morning at all: her breakfast is brunch. For this reason, among others, she has never had a full-time job for longer than a few months in an emergency, whereas I spent twenty years as a librarian, the last fifteen of them in the Foreign and Commonwealth Office in London.

The key to many of our differences lies in England, which has been my home for a total of forty years now. Much as I enjoy visiting my family in New Zealand, I feel like a tourist or, at times, a displaced person there. To use shorthand, I could never live permanently in a country with no medieval churches. I need history, ancient buildings and landscapes, and the northern cycle of seasons: real winters with Christmas in the middle, proper springs with Easter. I love ritual and traditions: sung Evensong with a cathedral choir and the language of Cranmer's prayerbook. I am obsessively fascinated by family history. My ideal day out might consist of driving off to some well-preserved village where our ancestors once lived, exploring the church, copying down inscriptions, and walking in the fields and

woods (preferably with a living member of the family). It would be May — hawthorn flowering in the hedges, bluebells in the woods. Marilyn also loves England, and would be a satisfactory partner in these pleasures; but if I may presume to describe her ideal day out it would be something like this: an afternoon spent wandering alone through well-stocked metropolitan shops, with frequent stops at coffee shops to sit and read her latest purchases, followed by a literary party or book launch in stimulating company, and then a meal in a restaurant. (If I am traducing her she will let me know.)

The settings in which I visualise her over the years flash past in a rapidly changing slide-show. Like our father, who was constantly moving house, she seems unable to send down roots in one place and stay put — whereas my mother and I, throughout all our travels over the last thirty years, have always kept one permanent base to go back to, hers in Mount Victoria, mine in East Finchley. I bought my house in 1967, in a street where I had been living since 1963. I have no mental pictures of Marilyn's backgrounds during the twelve or thirteen years of my first long absence from New Zealand, but they were various. When I returned to Wellington in 1975 she was living in Kelburn with Dan; the next time I came, after Dan's death, she was in Brooklyn with the children (one of his and two of hers — the others were grown up); then in the eighties she married and moved in with John; and now they have another house, nearer to the city. Once, when one of her daughters complained about the agonies of yet another shift, Marilyn told her, 'But it's fun to move house.' Fun! Endless tea-chests and packing and removal vans, fun? The spirit of our pioneer ancestors lives on in my sister.

Temporary moves can be fun, though; we both enjoy literary fellowships in towns or cities away from home, with only a few suitcases to transport, a flat to move into, and a new community to become part of. As well as these, Marilyn makes her own arrangements for refuges from everyday life: she writes her novels in a succession of other people's houses, doing duty as a cat-minder or plant-waterer while the owners are away. Everything stops when she is writing; often only her husband knows the telephone number. She works with total absorption, producing a new novel sometimes in a period of months. It fills me with amazement.

Because writing is a private activity I have seldom seen her actually doing it. In my visions of the adult Marilyn she is always doing something else — looking after children, for example, which filled years of her life. In 1962, when I was working at the Turnbull Library, she lived near me, and my Andrew used to go home from school with her little girls and stay until I finished work. Helen was six and the others five: an effervescent trio. Marilyn once rang me up at the library in a rage: 'Helen and Sarah have got ringworm — from that bloody hedgehog Andrew brought home!' (The spots turned out to be chickenpox, and no one's fault.) In more recent years she has made fairly frequent visits to England, and I see her there in several of my own settings: my house in London; my flat in Newcastle, where I had a fellowship for two years; Manchester, where we went on a pilgrimage to the scenes of our father's childhood after he died in 1987 — I have

photographs of her trudging through long grass in a derelict churchyard looking for our great-grandmother's grave; at a Faber party in London, her eyes glowing as she moved from group to group, talking to the likes of Julian Barnes.

By then she was thoroughly established in her second career as a writer; her first had come to an end when she found herself alone with four children, after the break-up of her second marriage. Dan, when she met him, had three children of his own, which left her no time for writing, but a year after his death she applied for the Katherine Mansfield Fellowship at Menton. Her elder daughters rallied round to help, and in 1980 she was able to escape to France and begin again. It is there that I see her, in one of the clearest vignettes in my mental portfolio. I went to stay with her in the tiny Katherine Mansfield Memorial room, sleeping on a mattress on the floor. She had so thoroughly taken on the coloration of her surroundings that she actually looked like some of the photographs of KM — her hair happened to be cut in a similar fringe, and her features did not contradict the impression.

But it is my first view of her, waiting for me on the little station at Garavan, that sticks in my mind. It was a fine warm day, and she was wearing a loose blue sundress with a frill around the hem, shaped (to my remembering eyes) rather like a bluebell. She came running along the platform to meet me, all sun-tanned arms and legs, healthy and joyful and healed. Now that really *was* a bluebell dance.

Renée

Poodle, Valerie Rose & Jimmy-the-Pumpkin

Renée was born in Napier, New Zealand, in 1929, and established herself first as a playwright, later as novelist. Her much-loved play *Wednesday to Come* was the first of a trilogy, which includes *Pass It On* (1986) and *Jeannie Once* (1990). She has also written radio plays and TV scripts. Her three novels are *Willy Nilly* (1990), *Daisy and Lily* (1993) and in 1995 *Does This Make Sense To You?* In 1989 she was Robert Burns Fellow at Otago University, Dunedin. She is currently working on a play, *A Certain Slant of Light*, and a novel, *The Snowball Waltz*. Her cat was recently interviewed for a forthcoming publication called *Household Gods*. She lives in Lower Hutt.

Once upon a time there were three kids, Poodle, Valerie Rose and Jimmy-the-pumpkin. Now there are two.

It is an evening in late May 1992 and we are having a cup of tea after a rehearsal of *Wednesday to Come* at the Globe Theatre, Dunedin. The question comes up, was Renée interested in theatre when she was young?

I wait for Val to say what I know, which is, apart from school things, not really. She surprises me.

Oh yes, Val smiles at the memory, Renée used to make my girlfriend Joy and me dance around waving a toetoe and singing Ramona and if we didn't do it to her satisfaction she'd belt us with the toetoe.

Everyone bursts out laughing. And after a moment's shock I do too. It is not the revelation of my bossiness. That is no surprise. It probably illustrates why I moved into directing in the theatre and why I'm not the kind of feminist who finds the process of consensus overwhelmingly attractive, although I have paid my dues. I was on the Broadsheet Collective. Perhaps I like to be where the buck stops. I was taught to be responsible, and try as I might, I can't break the habit. The difference between then and now is, I suppose, that I have realised I have a responsibility to myself too. I think Val learns that too.

But at this moment in the Globe Theatre I am startled because I have completely forgotten the incident about which Val speaks. Or incidents. Surely there has to be more than one such drama for it to stick in Val's memory. Doesn't there?

Memory is tricky. Memory changes. First there is the incident, the snapshot, the feelings at the time. Add the extra flesh that comes with superimposed retellings. Scrap the details that don't support your recall in the now. Memory is a paradox because, although false from the moment of inception, it does have an essential truth at its centre.

I am interested in this incident not only because of the lovely image of my sister dancing but also because it speaks to me across the years about Val's and my roles in our relationship when young. I am the oldest, therefore I am the boss. As a child my behaviour is modelled on Mum's — autocratic, authoritarian, never to be answered back.

This agreeable state of affairs is jarred out of its complacency one day when I slap Val for not doing things the way I think she should and she hits me back. I never touch her again except with affection. But the older sister–younger sister dynamic remains. When she wants to marry George she says he must ask me for permission and he does. Our mother is dead otherwise he would have asked her. George is a Southlander from Ohai. I don't know what he thinks of this. He looks just a little nervous but I am used to that. I have inherited from my mother the capacity to look formidable on occasions. Often underneath I am nervous or angry or unhappy or ill at ease or occasionally really feeling formidable and I get the look. My brother has it too. And Val.

I am aware as I write about my relationship with Val that my brother keeps popping into the story. I have decided to let him stay on the basis of accuracy. He was there when Val and I were young, when our relationship was being forged into the unbreakable bond it became, and he is part of it, although of course because he is male and we are female there are certain experiences, expectations, he wouldn't have, journeys he wouldn't make.

Ours, Val's and my, memories of each other and our mother, our brother, our childhood, are different because we each had our own particular mother, our own particular brother, although we call them by the same names and they look the same and in fact are the same people. So I, as writer of these pages, and you, as reader, have to be aware that this is a one-sided record because Val died on 28 September 1992, and cannot contribute her own.

Val has played bowls all day at the Tokoroa Bowling Club. George, her husband, with granddaughter Stacey, leaves home to pick her up but in the meantime Val has accepted the offer of a ride home. She waves and smiles goodbye to her friends and bowling colleagues and goes inside.

When George and Stacey arrive home the first thing George notices is the quiet. He calls out but tells me later, he knows then, in that moment, that there's something wrong. Val lies on the floor by their bed, her hand outstretched for the puffer she needs. Mouth-to-mouth is tried by the ambulance officer but Val is dead.

The phone rings in Dunedin. Bernadette answers it. It is Yvonne, Val's daughter. We both weep over the phone. I hang up. Bernadette and I cry, Val's visit in May–June pleasurably fresh in our minds although the last time I saw her is at my sister-in-law, Lillian's, funeral in late July and it is there one night we talk, the three of us, about how Val, Lillian and I used to sing

at parties and dances. *Sentimental Me, Too Young, Whispering Hope*, this last because it was a favourite of one of our aunties. I played (if you call using three chords for everything *playing*) the guitar accompaniment to these presentations.

My brother gets out photographs and there is a photograph of Lillian, Val and me draped in sheets with veils over our faces and lots of beads. A fancy-dress dance obviously. We remember incidents, the time years ago when my brother, in the euphoria of us all meeting again, drains his glass and throws it in the fireplace in the best Hollywood tradition. He's not a drinker so this is quite out of character. And the glass remains intact. Val and I giggle for hours and it has become a family joke, the sort of joke that only those who were there will appreciate. Val and I are great gigglers when we get together.

That night in my brother's kitchen we talk about all sorts of things but inevitably we end up talking about Mum. She was so little, Val says.

I think but don't say, but the Mum I knew was such a powerful presence, *is* such a powerful presence, in my life that physical size doesn't come into it when I think of her.

Now Val is dead.

Look after Val, Mum said.

Sure Val had chronic asthma, sure she had emphysema, although she'd never smoked but probably inhaled lots of mine in the days when I did, sure she had to be careful, but she's younger than me, for God's sake, and in May and June of just this year, just four bloody months ago, we do so much. Together we drive all over Dunedin, visit Larnach Castle and drool over the gardens, which even in the winter look great. Val takes a photo of Bernadette and me standing on the front steps in front of the castle. We visit the albatross colony. She loves Dunedin buildings. We have lunch at various cafés and restaurants. When we get home she writes in her notebooks.

This is the first time I know she keeps a record of her travels and experiences when she's away from home. We talk about journals and diaries and about Granna's notebook in *Wednesday to Come*. We laugh a lot. We always laugh a lot. We have the same sense of the ridiculous, the same liking for the throwaway line, the same attachment to the same family jokes. Remember the time old Gerry Wells sets fire to the fescue to burn it off and the fire gets out of control and we are all running round with damp sacks and Mum is swearing and Gerry has a heart attack and has to sit down under a tree and Mum tells him off? Typical, she says. Or the time Graeme Hamilton gets into difficulties swimming and his brother Ian dives in to help him, can't, and swims away yelling, I'm sorry Graeme, I have to save myself! Or the time we pinch dripping and potatoes and make a bonfire and cook the potatoes in one of Mum's Melrose tobacco tins and Bill and Carol and Mum come home from the pub and Bill nearly drives his old truck into the ditch because all they can see is the smoke billowing across the front of their place and they think it's on fire?

Val folds a large number of programmes for us while we are out at rehearsal. We scour the second-hand shops for props to dress the set. Together we go to a sale and buy some cheap teatowels. I have one of these in my hand when I answer the phone and it is Yvonne to say her mother, my sister, is dead.

She accompanies us to the Access Radio awards function, and the three of us get hysterical as we're driven, in the back of the stretch limo, to the Glenroy Auditorium. Us, in a stretch limo! Later Val writes in her notebook that the Sportsman of the Year Awards were being held next door to our function and a group of protesters were waiting for the Prime Minister to arrive and when we arrive in the limo they boo. Val also notes that Brett Shand and I scooped the pool for our show *SPANner in the Works* and lists our prizes. I read her comments and feel like young Jeannie in *Wednesday to Come*. Why are the radio, the award trophy, the tapes, still here when Val, so much more important to me, is gone?

Val (Valerie Rose) is born in 1931, the year of the big earthquake in Napier. I am eighteen months and my brother six months and Mum must have just fallen pregnant with Val when the earthquake struck late morning on 3 February. Mum, poor Mum, with us at her skirts, lives in a tent on Westshore Beach for some weeks.

Val is plump and pretty, dark shiny hair, dark brown eyes, pink cheeks. Much more beautiful than my dull all-over olive complexion. I love, resent, envy her. Mum cuddles her. I see myself bad-temperedly herding her and my brother to the lav down the path at the back of the little farmhouse cottage in Pakowhai from which my father leaves us forever when Val is two. He buys a .22 rifle, gets on the train, is found under the Thorndon railway bridge. Nobody, not even the police, know why.

While I wipe my brother's and sister's noses, accept responsibility for their behaviour, make sure they eat their tea, I observe my mother and uncles deal with this new situation. I hear my older uncle growl at his brother who is crying. For God's sake, that woman in there's got enough to put up with without listening to you. At the time all I know is that my father has vanished. I learn years later, after reading a newspaper report, that Mum takes my brother to the inquest in Wellington. I suppose she takes him for comfort, for someone alive to hold. I don't remember who looks after Val and me.

We can't stay in the farmhouse now there's no man there to do the job the house goes with, so we take rooms in a wooden villa in Guppy Road, Greenmeadows with Daisy, whose husband is in gaol and who needs the money, not to mention the company. At this time Daisy has, I think, three children, one of whom is a toddler and teaches himself to walk one day while Val and I watch, marvelling, as he falls over, picks himself up, staggers a couple of steps, falls again, chuckles at us, picks himself up, and eventually walks the whole length of the passage.

Mum knits us a new jersey every winter. Wool is sixpence a skein. She gets Val and me to wind the wool for her. We both want to wind, neither of us wants to hold the skein. My jersey is red, Val's is blue, my brother's dark green or maroon or grey, boy's colours.

Why can't I have blue?

Because you're dark, red suits dark people.

Can I have yellow?

Of course not. It will make you look too dark.

It is while we live with Daisy that Val meets Joy, who

becomes her best friend. At first Joy is younger and a drag who can't walk quickly enough and who grizzles when we and her four siblings deliberately leave her further and further behind as we walk to the river on hot summer days. Joy is triumphant when parents say we have to take her with us. We still run away from her, howls getting fainter as she becomes a dot behind us, then invisible. At some stage Val, who was born with a soft heart, and Joy become friends who giggle together until they can't stop and have to walk backwards into the long fescue so we can't see they are wetting their pants.

Val has a worn old teddy bear. I don't ever remember it new so maybe she was given it because someone had grown out of it or maybe we found it. Val loves that bear. His name is Edward Jones. For years she takes him everywhere except school. My brother and I tease her by throwing Edward up on the roof to make her cry.

Val is easy to make cry and there are times we enjoy provoking that. We all have nicknames. Mine is Poodle, Val's is Porky and my brother is Jimmy-the-pumpkin, Jimmy for short. My brother doesn't mind his so much but Val and I hate ours. I glower and glare, sulky and furious, refusing to speak, when I am called Poodle by anyone except my young uncle, whose pet I am (Jimmy is our older uncle's favourite and Val is our aunty's preference so it is all very fair) but Val hates Porky and is reduced to wild sobs by either my brother or me just outlining the word with our lips. I have grown much calmer about my nickname but I don't think Val would ever have been resigned to hers, which is dropped quite suddenly one day when my brother and I feel, without working it out till later perhaps, that there is something deeply unjust about hers. Porky evokes different feelings, nasty connotations, things that have nothing to do with Val.

When we are angry with Val she becomes Valerie and that is enough. The strong attachment between us is shaped by shared poverty, by necessity, by certainty that it's us against the world, but mainly by our mother. And this feeling, indestructible it seems, survives disagreements, rows, diverging views, differing perspectives, life changes, lifestyles, disappointments, successes.

Mum tells us that after my father's death she is advised to put the three of us in an orphanage so she can get on with her life but she thinks it would be wrong to do that. Another option offered is to go and live with her mother, who will look after us during the day while Mum goes out to work, but there is a history of anger, disappointment, a marriage 'out of the church', and now scandal, so my mother, being my mother, chooses a third, and hardest option, which is to keep us all together with her. Of course the bond between us is unbreakable.

Val and I share a double bed for some years then we have two single beds. We are always moving house either because landlords put up the rent to a sum Mum can't pay or the house we are renting is sold to someone who wants to live in it themselves. It would be the house in Moeller Street, Greenmeadows, where I belt Val and Joy with the toetoe.

We don't have a lot of furniture so we become very possessive about what we do have. I have a particular chair

which is mine and God help any kid who sits on it at meal times. Val also has a particular chair. We have 'our' knives and forks, spoons. Mum sits at the head of the table which is covered with the clean newspaper that serves as our tablecloth, the breadboard with the bread sitting on it, the bread saw to cut it and also to whack the backs of our hands if we reach for anything without asking permission or if we start 'fooling'.

Mum won't permit 'fooling' at the table. Or anywhere else. The moment we are finished eating she tells us to clear the table. As adults, Val, Jimmy and I still whisk plates and knives and forks and food off the table the moment it looks as though people have finished. Our kids are resigned to it but visitors and friends find it a bit odd to have their plates, cups and saucers raced away from them, especially if they've been saving that final piece of chicken or the last morsel of steamed pudding. And we do the dishes straight away as we were taught.

Mum gives us jobs. We take turns at the washing, wiping and putting away of the dishes. The washer-up is always leaving things to soak so that the next washer-up inherits horrible gluey-lined porridge pots or meat dishes with burned on fat around the corners. We moan and whine but Mum takes no notice unless we get too noisy about it.

We flick each other with wet teatowels and threaten revenge and retribution when our turn comes along. Val does the cooking on Sundays, I clean the house, my brother chops the wood and the kindling for the coming week and helps Mum dig the garden. We are all roped in for the weeding but

Jimmy and Mum do the most. And Jimmy and Mum weed carrots for Bill Hetherington for sixpence an hour. When I am twelve I leave school and go to work and with the money I give Mum and the money my brother has saved from his weeding efforts he pays for his uniform and books at Napier Boys' High. In the season he and Val cut asparagus for a man called Joe Wise down Guppy Road and they bring home asparagus and we eat it for breakfast with a poached egg on top and Val goes to Napier Girls'.

Mum teaches us to play euchre and five hundred and we fight over cards too.

You cheated!

I did not!

Mum, she cheated!

I did not!

I saw you take that card from kitty!

You're just jealous because your hand's no good!

Just because you think you're the world's best card player!

Better than knowing you're the worst!

Shut up you two.

Who are you telling to shut up?

You shut up!

Put the cards away.

Oh Mum.

It's all your fault!

Just another hand, Mum.

You heard me.

We sit around in the grass outside smoking the long dried fescue tubes. My brother farts. The next train down that

track'll be the goods, he says. Val and I laugh until we are nearly sick and she has to change her pants and wash the wet ones without Mum seeing. We remember this joke forever.

Val and I make our own paper dolls. We outline then cut out the cardboard bodies and colour in the faces. Then we make the wardrobe. We fight over colours, she rips one of my dresses, I grab Edward and squeeze his neck, she scrabbles for him, I throw him on the floor. See, I say, he's dead, hurray, Edward's dead!

Mum, Val screams, she's killed Edward!

I go into the shop where Mum has an account for groceries and put an orange on the bill. I do this every day for a month. Val shares the oranges. On pension day when I get home Mum is waiting. She has paid the bill, not let on that she didn't know about the oranges, but now she gets the dog collar down from the wall.

Did you eat any? she asks Val.

No!

I look at Val. I am incredulous. But I don't tell on her. Mum straps me hard. She is very angry. I scream and cry. When she is finished I run to my bed and sob into the pillow. I am not crying just because my bum and legs hurt.

I suffer the same shock of disbelief Mum feels when she sees the total and then reads the invoice to see why it is more than she expected. The worry of having to pay for extras not budgeted for from a store of money that is already very lean.

Val stands in the doorway. I glare at her. She looks sick. I don't speak to her for as long as I can hold out, probably a day.

I know why she did it, though. It wasn't so much that she was scared of being hurt but that she was scared of Mum's face when she knew that Val had done such a thing.

We all have characteristics that are listed by Mum when she's angry, when we haven't done our work to her satisfaction, when we've been lazy. I sulk, I answer back, I think I know everything, I'm devious, I've always got my head in a book. Jimmy sulks, has a temper, is not good at spelling, hangs around with his friends Lenny and Ray when he should be helping. Val sulks, is stubborn, cries at the drop of a hat over nothing, is too soft.

You'll be all right, Mum says, but if anything happens to me, you look after Val.

She says this to both me and my brother at different times. She cuddles Val because Val is more cuddly than me. I have always known this. I am jealous of Val because of this but I don't admit this for years after we have left childhood and then only to myself.

We go to learners' dances on Thursday nights at the Labour Hall in Taradale and we learn to foxtrot and waltz, memorise the steps to the Maxina, the Gay Gordons. We practise in the kitchen at Moeller Street. Each week we get better. The boys tie a hearth brush to the back of one of the adult's jackets and as he waltzes round and round the brush flies out in a wide arc and he doesn't feel it. Even the other adults laugh.

Val and I sew clothes on the old Singer treadle machine. She is better at it because she's prepared to take more time. Friday afternoons at school we have sewing. Val and I never

have the right materials so the teacher finds us some out of her box. We are shown how to sew a french seam, a double seam, hem, but first we all must make an oven cloth. A square of washed sugar sack, some coloured wools, a darning needle. There are pricked fingers, stitches that won't go right, impatience, tears, stitches still won't go right, impotence, fury, scissors handy, cut up the sacking. Big trouble. Eventually Val comes up with one she takes home. It's too thin, being only one layer of sugar sack, but doubled and quartered, it does.

We are two of the original marching girls when this sport begins and we go off with not too much grumbling to practices at Taradale Park at seven in the morning. We get the giggles from nervousness when the man teaching us bellows and spit shoots out. We shake silently and try not to let it show. I pray Val and Joy don't wet their pants.

We argue and fume at each other over the uniform. Every member has a different dream and each is loath to give it up. Economics rules as always. The Taradale Marching Girls haven't got much money. We end up with white sandshoes and socks, a maroon and white floral dress cut on princess lines and a white collar. Very prim. No flamboyance. No feathered hats, no boots, no military look. This is the early days. But we think we are Christmas.

Hope we get a pipe band. Pipe bands are better to march to on the street march. Our brother plays in the Port Ahuriri Caledonian Pipe Band. He has to practise on his chanter out in the woodshed. Mum can't stand the noise. He knows all about street marching.

On the day of the competitions we spend most of the time in the lav or waiting outside while one of us occupies the seat. Once the starting whistle goes we swing into action. We get nowhere on McLean Park. Our turns aren't crisp enough, one of us stumbles, we sweat and turn pale, our faces are taut with concentration, we forget all about keeping calm, looking as though we're enjoying ourselves, looking confident. Bugger all that, just get through it. Then never again.

We have a pipe band in front of us on the street march and get a third. We are ecstatic. That night there is a dance in the Foresters Hall in Dickens Street in Napier. At least we got somewhere. We can go in with our heads held high. We can feel sorry for those who got nowhere. We have a good time. We might not be the best team but we are the best dancers.

We play basketball, now called netball, in the C grade. Val, Joy and I play defence. We work well together except when we get snotty with each other over wild passes because we get too flurried or excited. Remember the tactics, we tell each other viciously, what the hell's the good of working out the tactics if we forget them when the heat's on? One year I am captain. Val is the tallest so when we have our team photograph taken in a line she is in the front. I am halfway and Joy is at the back.

We go away to Gisborne to play one weekend. We are billeted separately and I feel very frightened of the woman who billets me. I am scared of her hands which are crippled by arthritis. I dream those hands are opening my door, I see them sliding round the edge of the door. After I wake gasping

from this dream I lie awake for the rest of the night. In the morning I feel ashamed of myself. Poor thing. She can't help it. I tell Val and Joy. They have slept all night, happily, dreamlessly. You have to learn to control your imagination, says Val. For a while she and Joy amuse themselves crooking up their fingers and sliding them round doors at me. But we are growing up. The game palls quite quickly. And it's not right to make fun of people who really do have crooked fingers.

When I am nineteen and just married and Val is seventeen we stand in a hospital room and Mum, sick for two months from a cerebral haemorrhage, dies and the nurse puts the sheet over her face. Val screams, No! No! and faints, falling against me. Mum starts breathing again. The nurse nearly passes out on the bed with her. Mum lives another twenty-four hours. I am convinced she hears Val calling her and turns back from wherever she is, automatically. Because it is Val. They have a very strong bond. I am no longer envious or jealous, just nineteen and not knowing what to do. We have never seen death before.

We go and see Mum in the funeral parlour. She looks very still, very pale, very dead. Val faints again so I say she is not to go to the funeral service. I stay home with her so she won't be on her own. Later I regret this decision and wish we'd both gone.

When I am twelve Mum tells me the truth about my father's death. Until then I have this idea he died of pneumonia. Where that comes from I'll never know. Some book I suppose. I tell Val what Mum says to me about things she sees as my fault and I see very clearly that Val can't equate the Mum she knows with the Mum who says things like that. So we leave it.

Two days after Mum dies we get a letter from the landlord giving us notice. We don't know what to do. Just keep paying the rent, we are advised, and he can't put you out. Don't answer the letter, just go into Napier to the solicitors and pay the rent. So that's what we do.

Val and Jimmy live with my husband and me for a couple of years. She totes my first son around with her on the back of her bike. She loves him. He loves her. She works at Spackman's the chemist, in Napier, does all the developing of negatives and printing of photographs. She takes lots of photographs of the baby. This is why we have three times the photos of him than of the other two or Val's five.

She meets George at a dance at Bayview just before Christmas in 1948.

That was it.

She never looked at anyone else.

George works in Mangakino. Every Friday night he finishes work, gets washed and shaved and changed, shines his shoes then drives over the hard metal ups and downs, the loops, winding curves and steep drops, through the glaring sunshine, fog, snow, rain, wind of the Taupo Road and is outside Spackman's, waiting, at nine o'clock when Val knocks off.

George and Val get married on 22 December 1951. She is nineteen. They have five children. Val doesn't tell me about the last one because she's scared I'll tell her off for not using

contraception. So when I walk up her path and she's at the line, she comes towards me and bursts into tears. She's had the baby, it's quite small and has been kept in hospital and she's expressing milk to take up five times a day and she's nearly going mad and if I say anything she'll never speak to me again. I feel awful because my sister is frightened of me.

I sit down at her kitchen table and say if I ever said anything that made her believe it was any of my business how many kids she had or how quickly then I'm sorry and should have my tongue cut out. And her two eldest boys run round making a cup of tea. I can tell they've been told every time your Aunty sits down make her a cup of tea, she drinks a lot of tea. So Steve and Robin make tea for me. Constantly.

When the kids are older Val gets her driving licence and after a fortnight she drives the van on the bread run around the Mokai–Tihoi area over pumice, bog, in rain, sleet, you name it. Once she drives up a pile of metal in the fog — the fogs are deadly in that area — but she just puts the van into reverse and lets it gently, gently, slide back.

We both sew and knit furiously for our kids. Val also makes George's shirts. Val likes intricate Fair Isle knitting and I like complex patterns. Like me she is an avid reader. Like me she knits quite intricate patterns and reads at the same time. We both sing along to the radio when we think we're on our own.

We both work in our own grocery dairy, Val much longer hours than me because George is away on trucks and the shop opens at six in the morning because that's when the bread and milk is delivered.

She writes too, but in her notebooks, not for publication, and she writes good letters.

When we argue over the 1981 tour it is only partly about that. She is unhappy with the way my life is going. I have left my husband. She is very fond of him and he of her. We don't meet or correspond for nearly two years. Then, that soft heart again, she writes one of her letters and I am very happy to get it and I write back, send her a couple of *Broadsheets*, and it is like it was before. She has had eye trouble, an operation on her eye with only a local injection and I didn't know. How could I let that state of affairs continue?

She and George come and stay, Bernadette and I go and see them off when they go to Brisbane in 1987, we stay with them on our way to Dunedin. It's different but the same.

The first thing Val says when anything goes wrong or she is upset is never mind. Never mind she tells herself and me. Never mind.

She rings me. They say I've got emphysema. Don't know what I've done.

Don't know what I've done. A line that is so New Zealand I treasure it for its understatement, its pain, its anger, its stoicism.

Never mind, she says, never mind.

I don't think about her dying. Younger sisters don't die before older ones anyway. And she becomes secretary of the Tokoroa Women's Bowling Club for five or six years, treasurer for four, senior vice-president for two and is on her way to being president. We see each other but not often because I live in Dunedin.

There I find out things about my father and his family. I add these to the research I did many years ago on Mum's family. I tell Val each time and we don't talk about it a lot. What I find out merely confirms what we both thought so there's no real surprises.

I travel to Tokoroa for Val's funeral. I can't believe I am flying north for my sister's funeral. Bernadette has rung Geoff Walker at Penguin and told him my novel will be later than promised and he is very understanding. Life is imitating art. I am writing about death and how it affects my heroine Daisy. I can't believe she is gone.

George and I talk. Robin arrives and walks across the lawn to where I'm sitting on the front steps. He gets a shock. Thought you were Mum, he says and hugs me. Everyone else arrives. It's so soon after Lillian we are all in double shock.

We go and see Val. I see how her hands are crossed over each other, so still, so dead. It can't be true. Any minute she is going to wake up and start giggling.

Yvonne and I and her kids and a friend drive to the crematorium in Rotorua. We wait. Where is the hearse? The undertaker is very late. Finally he arrives, breathless, apologetic. A truck, overtaking on the wrong side, bangs into the front of the hearse. He has been held up getting names, addresses, details.

Trust Mum, says Yvonne.

We start to giggle and can't stop. Val's last joke. Knowing she would make us laugh. Certain Val is somewhere giggling her head off. For a few minutes our faces lose the strain, the unhappiness, the loss. We laugh, we hug each other, the kids laugh. Surprisingly, illogically, incongruously, we are happier than we've been for days. It doesn't last but it is enough to lift our spirits for these moments and on the drive back.

Today, three years later, when something funny happens I think how Val would laugh. I know I sound like her, look like her at some moments. I feel my face shift into one of her expressions. This is not because it's never happened before. It's just that since she died I have noticed it more. This likeness not so much of features but of a wry twist of the lips, a laugh, the way we walk. It could be unnerving but it's not. I like it.

Once upon a time there were three kids, Poodle, Valerie Rose and Jimmy-the-pumpkin. Now there are two. Never mind, I say to myself, never mind.